# Repertory with Roots:

## Black Youth, Black History, Black Culture, Black Music and the Bible

Ms Barbara,
For your loving support
I am grateful.
Continue to teach
our history, culture
music and the Bible
[illegible]
8/6/16

Richelle B. White, Ph.D.

Foreword by Anne E. Streaty Wimberly

xulon PRESS

*Repertory with Roots*
*Black Youth, Black History, Black Culture, Black Music and the Bible*
by Richelle B. White, Ph.D.

Printed in the United States of America.

ISBN 9781498476645



www.xulonpress.com

# Table of Contents

**Part 3: The Repertoire—Constructing a Pedagogy**



**Conclusion**



**Appendices**

# Dedication

To Black Youth Everywhere:

My prayer is that you will hunger and thirst after the one who has created you fearfully and wonderfully in his image. May you unashamedly and unapologetically embrace your identity as Black and Christian. Stand proud in the knowledge of who and whose you are.

In Honor of Pioneering Christian Educators,
Grant Shockley, Yolanda Smith, Anne Wimberly

There would be no Repertory with Roots without your groundbreaking, transformative and inspiring contributions to the field of Christian education. I stand on proud shoulders.
Thank you for blazing the trail.

Amen & Ashe

# Acknowledgements

I am thankful to many who have walked alongside me to bring this resource to completion. To my family, in particular my mother Patricia White Carroll, my Michigan mom Edna Simmons and my spiritual parents and mentors, Edward and Anne Wimberly who always believe in me. Thank you for support and holding me accountable and pushing me to put pen to paper even when I felt empty and exhausted.

To my Kuyper College family who always shows an interest in my writing projects, supports my work and inquires faithfully about my progress.

To my family at First Community A.M.E. Church especially the Daughters of Imani Rites of Passage ministry who excitedly engages and participates in my lessons that incorporate Black history, Black culture, Black music and the Bible. You push me to become a better teacher and communicator.

To my extended family and friends, thank you for your prayer support, words of encouragement and expressions of love as I labored and pushed this work into existence.

To my editorial team—Carrie Steenwyk and Dianne Zandbergen who served as proofreaders, formatters and caring supporters in the manuscript preparation process, I appreciate you.

My heart is overflowing with the grace that God has shown to me from conception to delivery of Repertory with Roots. Everywhere I turn God's grace is right there, and I am thankful. I am inspired by the faithfulness of Jesus in my life. His calling and purpose motivates me to press forward and use my gifts to serve others. The Holy Spirit's presence makes all the difference in who I am and what I do. To the triune God who is the architect of the universe and the creator of all, I give honor, thanks and praise now and always.

# Endorsements

In "Repertory with Roots: Black Youth, Black History, Black Culture, Black Music and the Bible," Dr. Richelle White powerfully clarifies underlying issues attacking the identity of Black youth and offers real and relevant strategies for teaching and learning that will develop Black youth as passionate disciples of Christ. In an engaging and deeply insightful manner she guides the reader through the process of designing curriculum that will help Black youth to find their identity through a transformative relationship with God.
Henry Bouma, Urban Youth Minister
The Navigators, Grand Rapids, MI

My professor while in graduate school began every class with the following quote, "No history, no self. Know history, know self." Though this quote was used to motivate the next class of social workers, this quote embodies the rich, thought- provoking work of Rev. Dr. Richelle White in "Repertory with Roots: Black Youth, Black History, Black Culture, Black Music and the Bible." Unfortunately, we live in a day and time when knowing one's self is connected to the number of likes received on Facebook, the number of retweets shared on Twitter and the number of followers on Instagram. If we do not teach our Black youth they are somebody because of their connection to the Kingdom of God, we will continue to perpetuate a vicious cycle of men and women that will look for their identity in all the wrong places. This work is needed, and furthermore, it is needed in your hands.
Rev. Kan'Dace L. Brock, LMSW
Fredricc Gerard Brock Ministries, San Antonio, TX

"Repertory with Roots" is an essential guide and must-read for anyone teaching youth in the Black Church. Dr. White has a unique way of provoking thought in the reader and the learner. If you are a Christian Educator looking to engage Black youth with their history, culture, music and the Bible to become an unapologetic disciple of Jesus Christ, I highly recommend this curriculum for your church and your personal library.
Rev. Zita Lee, Sunday School Superintendent
Abner Baptist Church, Glen Allen, VA

"Repertory with Roots" is unapologetically Black and offers a relevant and comprehensive socio-historical examination and considerations for working with today's Black youth. Dr. Richelle White has created a culturally relevant blueprint for aiding youth workers and other adult professionals in discipling Black youth within a culturally competent faith lens.
Jevon Willis, LLMSW, Associate Director
Grand Rapids Initiative for Leaders, Grand Rapids, MI

# Foreword

As I began to read this book, *Repertory With Roots: Black Youth, Black History, Black Culture, Black Music, and the Bible,* I was reminded of Dr. Richelle White's many years of ministry with and on behalf of Black youth. I recalled my numerous conversations with her about God's call and her response to it to serve the young as well as to provide guidance to others who must take up the mantle of youth ministry leadership or become able spiritual companions along the way. Her remarkable contributions to the field of youth ministry came to mind including the contextually relevant, Bible- and life-based resources on mentoring: *Daughters of Imani—Planning Guide: Christian Rites of Passage for African American Young Women* (2005) and *Daughters of Imani—Young Women's Bible Study* (2005) in addition to her decade -long leadership of and curriculum development for high school youth in the Youth Hope-Builders Academy (YHBA) , a theological program for high school youth sponsored by Interdenominational Theological Center, which I direct. In both her face-to-face ministries, teaching, and published resources, Dr. White has consistently been a powerful voice and promoter of contextually relevant, biblically-based, and theologically sound approaches. She has maintained a vital concern for what is real in the lives of Black youth, and what is necessary for them both to survive and thrive. So, it did not come as a surprise that she has continued her lifelong calling in this new offering.

There is no doubt that this book comes at a tough time in the sojourn in the United States of Black people in general and Black youth in particular. The question Dr. White poses and provides guidance to engage youth in answering, "What does it mean to be and live as unapologetic Christians and unashamed Black persons?" comes in this Post-Christian era of waning influence of the Christian faith all around us, the growing incidence of biblical illiteracy, Black youth's disconnection from the past, and their presence in a broken Black cultural "village". She is quite right in naming the rituals of mourning that result from the day-after-day killings of our youth by one another, by law enforcement, and others on the streets within and outside our communities. There is no denying our youths' wrestling with self-esteem, health issues, and their dealing with struggles at home, in schools, in the juvenile justice system, and in the community at large. There are increasing numbers of Black youth who are disconnected from organized religion, while at the same time, it is appropriate to say that our churches are disconnected from them. The news in this highly dangerous, de-villaged, technologized and commercial world in which we live is that our youth have become what Dr. Edward Wimberly (2000) calls "relational refugees" , or persons who are disconnected from significant relationships. From where I sit, there is a deafening cry for hope amidst hopelessness and a way to move from the weeping that lingers over the night to joy in the morning (Psalm 30:5b). Yet, the ancillary question is: "What, precisely, are the ways that can actually move youth and the adults in their lives in the direction of hope and joy? Dr. White extends an important and necessary invitation to us to engage young people in what may be called an essential hope- and joy-directed repertory grid.

My particular use of the term, "repertory grid" builds on, yet takes a somewhat divergent direction from the early work of George A. Kelly in *The Psychology of Personal Constructs* (1955, 1963) and its updated reprint, *The Psychology of Personal Constructs* (1991). The repertory grid methodology utilizes multiple constructs that assist persons' examining, perceiving, and making sense of the world they live in and determining the direction of their journey forward. I see in Dr. White's extraordinary book, an immensely helpful repertory grid methodology that she appropriately calls "engaged pedagogy". In it, she guides leaders in immersing young people in the enlivening constructs of our African cultural past that form a source for positive ethnic-racial identity; Black American historical values that are to be honored and mirrored in the lives of our young; the variety of Black music genres that call for critical assessment of values to be accepted or rejected; values clarification found in the principles of Kwanzaa; and Biblical texts that raise critical questions for today and provide faith basics for today's and tomorrow's sojourn of life. Her concern is squarely on young people's wisdom formation that is anchored in Christian belief, their understanding of what constitutes moral action reflective of Christian spirituality, and their engagement in the spiritual disciplines through which Christian discipleship is grounded and nourished.

At this point, I want to draw attention to four key features of the book that are particularly salient for ministry with Black youth and, for that matter, with all youth today, as well as for those who lead them. The first is the realness of her methodologies found in her repeated insistence on the voices of the youth. A dominant critique of today's youth is that adults including in our churches neither see them nor hear them. The impact of this on Black youth is astronomical because of their persistent invisibility and muteness in wider society. Dr. White's uses of questions throughout the lessons found in the Appendices not simply highlight the means of eliciting the voices of youth, but also the processes by which their agentic selves are affirmed, nurtured, and set forth in meaning-making endeavors.

Second, Dr. White's insertion of her own personal stories both highlight and model for leaders the value of the self-disclosure of spiritual companions. I find great affinity with this activity because it calls to mind my own experiences and uses of it in what I refer to as creating a spiritual companion journey alongside youth. Self-disclosure opens the way for inviting the stories of young people; and in fact, it helps to create a safe space for theology-as-conversation or for forming *holy ground* where up- close and personal connectedness of young people's everyday stories with the canonical story and stories from the past and through the artistic medium of music can be fostered. *Holy ground* begets *holy conversations* where the tough questions can emerge, "Who am I?" "Why was I born?" "Why is life so tough?" "What's going to happen to me?" "Is there really a God who listens and cares?" In a real sense, the self-disclosure of leaders or spiritual companions of youth that opens the way for open conversation with youth embodies the biblical model of Jesus Mentorship with his disciples. Jesus was the up-close and personal guide and spiritual companion who posed real questions about life, heard the questions of his followers, and engaged in conversation about the answers.

Third, the call in the resource for intergenerational and family interaction and connectedness goes a long way in promoting "village" healing. It affirms that young people are not given over to their peer groups to "raise them". Neither are they left alone to "figure out" life in general and answers to the deep questions of faith and life. At the same time, Dr. White is quite right in stating that adults themselves can benefit from their co-engagement with young people.

Finally, there is critical need for resources that tell *what* is needed that can result in Black youths' claiming themselves and living as unapologetically Christian and unashamedly Black and *why* it is needed. But, this resource goes the extra step in demonstrating *how* to do it. The provision of concrete interactive steps in lessons aimed toward belief formation, ethical embodiment, theological grounding, character development, and historical-cultural enlightenment is a profound gift.

Indeed, I have received this resource as a gift and reckon it as a gift to be shared and used for the essential work of ushering in God's promise of hope to youth in an age of distress and making possible joy in the morning for them and us all.

Anne E. Streaty Wimberly, Ph.D.
Executive Director, Youth Hope Builders Academy
Professor Emerita, Interdenominational Theological Center, Atlanta, GA

## Introduction

# Repertory with Roots: What is it? Why the Church Needs It

Jasmine had just finished reading the case study, "Left Speechless," which talks about the challenges of living as an unapologetic Christian in today and tomorrow's world.

Ms. Janine, the teen girls' rites of passage program director asked the group, "What's an unapologetic Christian?"

Tamara raised her hand and said, "Someone who's not afraid to stand up and live for Christ. Someone who is being real with it— Christ, that is. They ain't faking it."

"O.K., I hear you Ms. Janine responded. "Would that be you?"

"Oh, I ain't saying all that. But I'm trying," Tamara countered.

The dialogue and discussion continued as the students debated what they believe, what they accept as true, and how to grow stronger in their convictions. The intriguing conversation led to more questions. Ms. Janine wanted to explore a specific section of the case study where Roderick, a Black Muslim attempts to convert Shawna, a Christian.

> Roderick continued, "Sister, it's time for you to wake up and see the light, the Master Wallace Fard Muhammad, he is the Messiah, Jehovah, God, the Son of Man. He came to bring life to his mentally and spiritually dead people, the African Americans. Our Savior, Wallace Fard Muhammad came to bring a world of peace and righteousness built on the foundation of truth and justice. Sister, now you have heard the truth. The truth will set you free. I guess I got carried away. Did you want to share something about what you believe?"

After re-reading this section, Ms. Janine asked the group, "What is wrong with Roderick's beliefs?"

Following a lengthy pause, Samantha responded, "There is nothing wrong with what he believes, he didn't have to say what he said in the way that he said it."

"What do you mean by that?" Ms. Janine asked.

"It's the way he said it. Like he had an attitude, he can believe what he wants to believe, he doesn't have to get smart about it."

Ms. Janine hoped that her face did not show the "shock" that she felt. A young believer who does not see anything wrong with another person claiming to be Christ was not only problematic but stemmed from a greater problem that people in our churches, particularly young people are confronting. People do not know what they believe and why.

This slice of a meeting of a Rites of Passage and mentoring program for African American[1] middle and high school girls is indicative of the postmodern influence that permeates society and infiltrates the hearts and minds of students. It demonstrates the difficulties they experience when confronted with being able to distinguish God's truth from the world's lies.

Upon closer examination of this case, a couple of things should cause grave concern. First, students can define and affirm the definition of an "unapologetic Christian," yet fail to seek it as a non-negotiable way of life for a believer. Second, a student can believe in Christ and not see anything wrong with another human being making the claim of being Savior of the world.

These realities are alarming because they indicate a double-mindedness that James speaks about in the first chapter of his letter to the twelve tribes. James says, "Dear brothers and sisters when troubles of any kind come your way, consider it an opportunity for great joy. For you know that when your faith is tested, your endurance has a chance to grow. So let it grow, for when your endurance is fully developed, you will be perfect and complete, needing nothing. If you need wisdom, ask our generous God, and he will give it to you. He will not rebuke you for asking. But when you ask him, be sure that your faith is in God alone. Do not waver, for a person with divided loyalty is as unsettled as a wave of the sea that is blown and tossed by the wind. Such people should not expect to receive anything from the Lord. Their loyalty is divided between God and the world, and they are unstable in everything they do."[2]

The youth of today including and specifically Black youth are facing trials. Peer pressure, the death of unarmed Black youth by law enforcement, issues of beauty and body image, living into stereotypical identities perpetuated by the media, the realities of racism and prejudice, and questions about God and faith permeate the minds of youth. They are asking why God allows all of this to happen. Why does life have to be so difficult? How do they live with all of this suffering going on around them? James teaches that prayer and the wisdom of God are the tools needed to navigate the treacherous terrain youth are forced to climb.

For more than 30 years I have been building relationships with African American youth through my work in the public school system, churches, parachurch organizations, community partnerships and various other arenas. The youth that I have encountered on a personal level have revealed two important ideas regarding having a personal relationship with God: 1) they do not like "fake Christians," and 2) if they can't be real with God it's best to "fall back". I have embraced the term unapologetically Christian, introduced and made popular by the Trinity United Church of Christ in Chicago as a means of representing who we are as African American Christians. The expression unapologetically Christian as defined by Tamara, one of the students in the aforementioned case study is "someone who's not afraid to stand up and live for Christ. Someone who is being real with it, Christ that is. They ain't faking it."

In terms of living this way, Black youth tend to think that living an authentic Christian lifestyle is something that they can practice when they are older. They know what an unapologetic Christian is, but do not embrace it as a way of life during their adolescent years. Some reasons for waiting include—"not being able to enjoy life or hang out with my friends, not being able to do what my peers are doing because I feel like God is always watching, and I'm not ready to give 100% right now, God might interfere with my plans." If youth don't feel like they can be real with God, they are likely to fall back. Falling back is a phrase used by young people to denote someone who should back up or cool down. Several youth that I have encountered have often said, if they can't commit to God 100 percent, then they're not going to fake it. They continue to usher or sing in the choir, but telling others about Jesus and testifying or witnessing is not what they want to do during this time, so falling back becomes their modus operandi. Their method of operation becomes a religious routine that they fail to see as "faking it," a way that they tend to despise. As stated before, this is an example of double-mindedness, which James delineates as leading to instability in all things.

The second area of grave concern highlighted from the case study is being a believer in Jesus Christ and not seeing anything wrong with another human being making the claim of being Savior of the world. In reviewing the case study, Samantha had no problem with Roderick's beliefs of proclaiming Wallace Fard Muhammad as the Messiah, Jehovah, God, the Son of Man. Rather, she thought the problem was with his attitude. Samantha is more concerned with issues of respectability, not issues of faith and belief. Her convictions about respect are stronger than what she believes. This is a pure indication of the postmodern philosophy at work. Postmodernism emulates religion as a matter of personal taste and individual choice, thus the statement "there's nothing wrong with what he believes." Each person is "free" to choose what he or she believes for themselves because faith is relative, embracing a personal standard of belief that suits his or her tastes. Perhaps the most shocking idea related to Samantha's proclamation is that she is an active member of a church that uses the Decalogue (Ten Commandments) as a standard component in worship each Sunday. The Decalogue begins with " I am the Lord Your God, who brought you out of the Land of Egypt, out of the house of slavery, you should have no other gods before me." Nothing wrong with Roderick's beliefs, in light of the commands from the Decalogue, frightening thought.

The implications of knowing the calling to live as committed and authentic disciples but doing otherwise and accepting beliefs that are contradictory to Christian values are far reaching and must be addressed by relational, real and relevant forms of Christian education and youth ministry. A term that young people often use when adults are "living" contradictory lives before them is the label hypocrite, which can be defined as a person who engages in the same behavior that he or she condemns others for. When a young person confesses Christ, yet fails to live out the commands of Christ, he or she can be likened to a hypocrite as well. However, due to characteristics of adolescent development, namely the inability for complex and abstract thinking, youth are unable to identify that as problematic. If a young person is not able to pinpoint the discrepancies, then it is the responsibility of youth pastors, youth workers, Bible study instructors, Sunday school teachers and other committed adults to teach them and facilitate learning processes that will assist in their holistic (physical, emotional, social, intellectual, spiritual) growth and development.

Finding nothing wrong with another person who claims to be the Savior of the world is not only problematic but frightening as well. A modern proverb, by an unknown author says, "If you don't stand for something, you will fall for anything."[3] Calling oneself a Christian yet not standing for Christ and distinguishing between the truth and a lie when a man exalts himself as the Christ such as seen in the case study indicates the use of feelings rather than reason and conviction to make her decision. Samantha in the opening account felt disrespected, and because that was the case, she responded with her emotions, not her reason. Because her emotions were entangled, Samantha could not differentiate. Because Roderick spoke with an attitude, she felt disregarded. Samantha was so consumed by her feelings and emotions that she neglected to absorb the message. Christian apologist Ravi Zacharias offers this comment about the postmodern generation; they listen with their eyes and think with their emotions.[4]

For more than 10 years, I have developed, refined and redefined the Repertory with Roots Pedagogy of Engagement. It is my conviction that the model has the potential to address the aforementioned problems as well as the Black church's challenge of seeing, reaching, hearing and engaging Black youth. I would like to call our attention to a very important passage in scripture that outlines how young people should live their lives as unapologetic Christians. 1 Timothy 4: 12 reads, "Don't let anyone look down on you because you are young, but set an example for the believers in speech, in conduct, in love, in faith and purity." I have often heard this passage preached at Youth Day Celebrations, in fact I have preached it myself in hopes that it would motivate youth to set examples for their peers in the areas of speech, conduct, love, faith and purity. However, I missed the mark, because I was preaching at, rather than inviting youth to walk together and alongside adults who were modeling what Paul was sharing with Timothy.

I have been blessed to walk alongside young people as a teacher, mentor, friend, spiritual mother and confidante. I journey with them as others have journeyed with me and paved the way for my growth and success. God has allowed me to meet and do life with so many people who have poured into my ministry and afforded me educational opportunities that have changed my life. These experiences have given me the chance to preach and teach in the Body of Christ locally, nationally and internationally. This multiplicity of experiences and opportunities has prepared me to share the gift of *Repertory with Roots: Black Youth, Black History, Black Culture, Black Music and the Bible*. It is written with both youth and their leaders in mind. It is for those who want to join the movement of walking in a new vision of seeing, reaching, hearing and engaging Black youth.

*Repertory with Roots: Black Youth, Black History, Black Culture, Black Music and the Bible* is a pedagogy of engagement whose goal is to educate for discipleship, specifically Christian wisdom formation. It is a model of teaching focused on connecting teaching and learning with the overall experiences of Black youth. It introduces a skillfully developed model of teaching that meets youth in their historical, cultural, and musical contexts. It moves beyond the prevailing comfort zone of Black churches, offering relational, real and relevant ministry with Black youth. ***Repertory with Roots* is a designated ontological niche wherein lies sources for African American youth's identity formation. This niche is comprised of but not limited to four important elements—Black history, Black culture, Black music and the Bible.** These four elements are encapsulated into a holistic educational framework that educates as discipleship for Christian wisdom formation. This pedagogical framework possesses the potential to assist in the holistic development of African American youth because it fosters seeing, reaching, hearing and engaging them in a manner that fosters movement toward being authentic, unapologetic disciples of Jesus Christ.

Jesus was not a Christian; he was the Christ. He did not attend worship on Sunday, Bible study on Wednesday, and Youth group on Friday. Yet, he is revered as the founder of the Christian church. Christ's church welcomes all who confess Christ as Savior and Lord. Christ's church welcomes those who love God, neighbor and self. The intricacies of Christ's commands are delineated in the Word of God. The doors of Christ's church should swing on welcome hinges for all who desire to grow in the knowledge of God, Jesus Christ and the Holy Spirit. However, young people are not always treated this way. Before the church even came into existence, Jesus found himself defending and encouraging young people before his disciples and others. The Gospel writer Mark, shares the story in this way: "The people brought children to Jesus, hoping he might touch them. The disciples shooed them off. But Jesus was irate and let them know it: 'Don't push these children away. Don't ever get between them and me. These children are at the very center of life in the kingdom. Mark this: unless you accept God's kingdom in the simplicity of a child, you'll never get in.' Then gathering the children up in his arms, he laid his hands of blessing on them."[5]

Don't push them away! At the very center of life in the Kingdom! You'll never get in! These words spoken by Jesus when the disciples tried to shoo the children away, demonstrate that He sees, hears, reaches and engages youth. He calls the Church of God to do the same through building relationships, creating programs, and writing curriculum that informs, engages and motivates young people to live godly lives. *Repertory with Roots* is a teaching/learning resource that nurtures the aforementioned calling of the church. It focuses its attention on the African American experience building on cultural awareness and identity development. Through committed and faithful efforts in using this pedagogical framework Christ's body can be strengthened by developing a strong and knowledgeable army of young people who desire to live and serve Christ.

If the church is to be relevant, senior pastors, youth pastors, youth workers, Bible study teachers, Sunday school teachers and other committed adults must believe that Christian education is vital to the work of the Black church. And Christian education must reflect a commitment to build a program that is relational, real and relevant: it must be excellent in its implementation and execution. Following this view, *Repertory with Roots* considers the unique learning needs and contexts of African American youth through engaging youth by providing opportunities for them to listen to African American lyricists, poets and orators—allowing space to learn based on the contributions of each member of the group, and encouraging open discussions about Christian beliefs, the Bible and application of those beliefs to their lives. Through an exploration of shared values, youth are encouraged to walk out what they talk about, becoming living examples of their beliefs. Christian education on these terms builds and strengthens the church. Join me on this journey to do just that. In three part harmony we will explore I) Black Youth: The Roots and Sources of Identity; which explores the roots that shape African American youth identity—Black history, Black culture, Black music and the Bible; II) The Vision: Relational, Real and Relevant; describes theoretical foundations of a vision of holistic ministry for, with and by Black youth; and III) The Repertoire: Constructing a Pedagogy delineates how *Repertory with Roots* educates for Christian wisdom formation through experiential teaching and learning sessions.

In short, Black youth identity is integral to their development as Christians. Envisioning the possibilities for transformative Christian education that helps Black youth declare "I am unashamedly Black and unapologetically Christian," should motivate the church to step up and intentionally identify ways to see, reach, hear, and engage Black youth with their history, culture, music and the Bible.

# Part 1

# Black Youth—The Roots and Sources of Identity

## Chapter One

# Foundations—Black Youth and Identity "Knowing Who and Whose You Are"

*"True identity theft is not financial. It's not in cyberspace. It's spiritual. It's been taken."*[6]

Several years ago, I became aware of identity theft. The idea that someone out in cyberspace could fraudulently acquire and use my private identifying information for financial gain frightened me. I, like other hardworking Americans, feared that my personal and financial information would be compromised and my hard earned money would be lost. Thoughts of credit card theft and misfiled income tax returns in my name became a source of paranoia. How would I protect myself? Sometime later, I was watching TV and an advertisement for Lifelock Identity Theft Protection Services flashed across the screen. Their tag line read "every identity deserves protection."[7]

This service promised a solution to my problems of fear and paranoia. They promised to monitor my credit score and credit card accounts. I would be notified of any suspicious activity regarding the use of my personal information. My identity would be protected. I called Lifelock, and spoke to a representative who reassured me that I was making a wise decision. Long story short, I enrolled in Lifelock Identity Theft Protection Services. After a time, I realized that this was a service I did not need because I was not at high risk for identity theft. I spent a substantial amount of money for a service that was unnecessary. I believed the hype. I bought into the lie. "I had been hoodwinked, bamboozled, led astray, run amuck" (in my Denzel Washington voice from the movie *Malcolm X*). I believed that my identity was tied to financial resources. I believed that if my monetary income was taken from me that I was less valuable. I had tied my identity to temporal things which come and go. The lesson I learned: Identity is more than possessions and material things.

Identity is a reflection of God's image and God's character in a person's life. Genesis 1:27 says "God did just that. He created humanity in his image. Created them male and female.".[8] We, each of us are created in God's likeness, uniquely designed to be an impression of God. Each person's unique; one-of-a-kind fingerprint reveals that.

Identity is also connected to purpose and knowing who you are. The question; "Who am I?" is one of the fundamental questions of adolescence. Teens are searching for a source of meaning; they want to know who they are and why they were created in the first place. Returning to my story about identity theft, I was left wondering how I got trapped into seeking a false identity. How did I buy into the lie that my worth could be tied to finances? In trying to protect my American dream, I almost forgot about the giver of the dream—the triune God. As I looked at my checkbook and the money I was wasting, I came to myself and canceled my subscription to Lifelock.

**Identity Thieves**

As I encounter Black youth, I witness that they too are buying into the lie. Society encourages materialism and materialistic attitudes among youth through the media and advertising. Some put their identity in clothes, money or possessions. Others lean on success to define who they are. Some youth depend on other people, specifically those they are dating. Youth, both male and female, are pressured to achieve physical perfection. The media has become an equal opportunity discriminator as it relates to body image.[9] These things— clothes, money, possessions, success, dating relationships and body image—can be described as identity thieves.

When some young people do not have access to name brand clothing they experience feelings of insecurity because they believe that others will not accept them if they are not wearing "designer clothes." When youth do not succeed at what they are trying to accomplish, the failure greatly affects them because they are placing their identity in success. Competing on athletic teams and in the classroom for scholarship opportunities produce great amounts of stress, anxiety and pressure to succeed. Youth who tie their performance to identity begin to question who they are. Youth who are looking for their identity through dating relationships face difficulties when there's a break-up.

By placing unrealistic expectations on Black youth, the media is telling them that they cannot be themselves and they have to "fix" what they look like. These identity thieves walk alongside Black youth every day. As Steven Covey says in the opening quote, identity theft is spiritual. There is a spiritual identity crisis that is consuming youth across socio-economic, educational, personal, social, emotional and cultural lines.

This spiritual identity crisis as Cornel West argues cannot be ignored. We need spiritual resources to be empowered politically and economically. [10] Identity theft is seated at the very core of their being. It is hijacking their spirituality. Identity thieves are enticing Black youth to forsake their individuality as African American Christians. It is drawing youth away from their spiritual identity as unashamedly Black, unapologetically Christian youth who are divinely destined to serve.[11]

One thing I have learned throughout my life is that someone can take something from you, and you may not be aware of it. For example, when I was growing up as a teenager in suburban Philadelphia, my cousin and I would spend the weekends together. On one occasion, she took my lunch money and I did not know it. She went into my room when I was not there and took my money out of my wallet. I realized my money was missing when I went to pay for my lunch on Monday at school. Similarly, some of us have been robbed of our identity. We have been robbed emotionally, physically, intellectually, socially, or spiritually, and we don't even know it until we need to draw on those resources as sources of strength, encouragement, insight, wisdom or power. This is how identity thieves work to destroy Black youth. Young people may be unaware of the people, places, or things that are seeking to steal, kill and destroy their identity. Their spirituality, self-esteem and other areas of their life are being systemically seized. Therefore, it is important that pastors, youth workers, counselors, teachers, mentors, advocates and others stand in the gap by praying, teaching, training, affirming, mentoring, encouraging and engaging Black youth in identity building activities to address the crisis that is seeking to annihilate African American youth.

### Identity: Internal and External Influences

Identity has both internal and external influences. Internal identity refers to the traits we ascribe to ourselves, and external identity denotes what the outside world thinks of us. Internally, there are words and images that represent how we describe ourselves. Externally, the words and images of others represent how we think others view us and label us. This view of identity manifests in a person's self-esteem. Some of the factors that shape self-esteem include family, community, the media and peers. Oftentimes, youth look beyond family to see where they fit in the world, and sometimes they believe that they do not have a place at all. This feeling of displacement serves as a contributing factor that shapes who a young person is. These factors are culprits for feelings of low self-esteem, which potentially lead to the inability to dream, a lack of purpose, a loss of hope. Constant put-downs, critical comments, bullying, and media prevent Black youth from seeing themselves as valued creations of God; this leads to a poor overall evaluation of self.

Another external influence on African American youth identity is music. Black music serves as a central influence regarding values and making sense out of life. Much of what Black youth listen to cannot be classified as spiritually inspirational but includes messages that are problematic and harmful to Black youth's self-esteem. Hip-Hop often fits that description. Some messages in Hip-Hop music negatively influence adolescent sexual views, desires and behaviors. Educational therapist Michael Porter asserts that African American youth are eroticized through their exposure to negative rap lyrics and videos.[12]

This means that their sexuality is being manipulated by the lyrics, video images and personalities of the Hip-Hop industry. These identity thieves are at work, twisting and distorting the image of God which is foundational to Black youth identity.

Let me clarify, not all Hip-Hop artists and music diminish the image of God. I offer three broad categories that represent the history of rap music for consideration—status, progressive and gangsta rap. Status rap consists of boasts, arrogance and mild significations, argues for African American inclusion in material wealth.[13] Status rap explicitly discusses the social aspects of life. An example would be rap's first commercial hit, "Rapper's Delight," recorded in 1979. Progressive rap is the next category that I will define. Progressive rap is socially conscious rap. In 1982, Grandmaster Flash and the Furious Five released "The Message." It became one of the most influential and significant rap singles of all time.[14] As it developed, progressive rap began to critique the social, economic and political factors that led to its inception and development. Those factors include drug addiction, police brutality, teen pregnancy and other forms of material deprivation.[15] As progressive rap developed, Long Island rap group Public Enemy came on the scene. Their music was directed toward an explicitly self-aware, pro-black consciousness. They consider themselves to be preservers of the Black mind.[16] The third category gangsta rap is characterized by Black on Black gun violence, Black male-female relationships, women-hating, sexual violence and extreme individualism which reinforce images of the sex-violence worldview. The worldview of gangsta rappers is problematic because of its derogatory messages; however, it continues to be popular among Black youth because it is considered to be authentic in the sense that it emanates directly from the streets and does not disguise its messages. It delivers a message of a "gritty reality" of the life in the inner city. Rap and Hip-Hop continue to have major influence among African American youth. However, the key is to create space and place for youth to constructively dialogue and think critically about rap and Hip-Hop.

## Who are Black youth? What are Their Experiences?

Being Black is a unique cultural experience because of an African past and an American present and future. The history and spirituality of Black people begins with Africa. Understanding "Africa" through the lens of African culture, we tend to formulate general impressions of what it means to be of African descent. Wherever African diasporic people live, African culture is present. This can be affirmed as living history. It is important that Black youth become aware of their rich historical and cultural heritage. However, this becomes difficult when media portrayals override making sense of pride and honor. The consistent images of starving children who can be supported for less than a dollar a day bombard the television, which gives the impression that Africa is racked with famine and poverty. Seeing these images constantly fuel the assumption that Africa has had no influence on the history of the world or the development of western culture.[17] In order to develop a positive African identity, Black youth must be taught to view Africa, African culture and African people from a place of creative strength. An accurate interpretation of African history and culture through personal and communal experience is integral. Exposure in this way moves youth in the direction of embracing their African identity because they can more accurately see where they have come from.

In addition to Black youth interpreting their identity as Africans is the necessity of viewing themselves as Americans as well. If Black youth were to only ground their identity in America, it would force them to connect with the "slave identity." Connecting in this way, results in Black Americans being tethered to a false identity –the slave identity. When Africa is excluded from the beginnings of Black people, the term African American consciously and unconsciously becomes a synonym for the powerless, hopeless, helpless and degraded Black person in America.[18] Moving from this perspective requires all Black Americans, young and old, to liberate themselves from the slave identity. Examining the great repository of accomplishments of African Americans before and after emancipation provides inspiration, creativity, determination, hard work and a source of strength. Knowing who and whose you are can empower Black people, especially Black youth, to transcend the crucible of the slave mentality and build a better world for themselves and generations yet unborn.

Although the history and culture as Africans in America is rich, Black youth still waver in their identity as African Americans, due to racism and racist attitudes. Black youth's understanding of racism as racial prejudice is oftentimes equated with perceived injustices perpetrated by white people. This comes from personal experience as well as from the media. The minds of Black youth are assaulted daily by media culture that promotes white people as superior, which maintains attitudes of white supremacy. bell hooks says that television socializes Black youth to believe that their subordination should be considered the norm because most Black characters are portrayed as a little less ethical and moral than white characters.[19]

This attitude is fueled by stereotypes. Stereotypes refer to a generalization, usually exaggerated or oversimplified and often offensive, that is used to describe or distinguish a group.[20] Color prejudice and racism in the form of stereotypes have existed for a long time in the United States.[21] Stereotypes play a significant role in the lives of Black youth as they make sense of what it means to be African American. The significance of negative stereotypes impacts their lives greatly. Black youth are stereotyped physically, psychologically, intellectually, socially, physically and emotionally in classrooms, on the movie screen, and in a variety of other places. Black youth on all levels are denigrated in the media. Others are shot dead in the cold for wearing a hoodie or listening to loud music. Black youth suffer ridicule and embarrassment because of stereotypes. The generalizations related to color and culture fractures Black youth identity. It robs them of the opportunity of living with personal and racial authenticity and integrity. So, how do we mend these fractured identities? My offering is to teach African American history and culture, impart the values of Black self-love and cooperation, and most importantly teach them about their identity in Christ.

## Finding Their Identity in Christ

As stated previously, a person's identity is directly connected to their purpose. By helping youth understand who they are, we can help them to identify what they have been created to do. Through affirmations from the word of God, spiritual gifts and leadership inventories as well as other measures, we can join them on the journey to identity and purpose. Identity also joins with a young person's value and worth. If a teen's identity is not rooted in Christ, they can be compared to leaves on a tree blowing wherever the wind takes them. It is integral that we, pastors, youth pastors, youth leaders, counselors, teachers, mentors and advocates help youth to understand the necessity of placing their identity in Christ, our never changing creator and sustainer.[22]

I would identify five things that youth should believe concerning their identity and value.

1) **God created them intentionally in His image.** Out of all the things that God created from Genesis 1:1 – 2:1, he only formed human beings in His image and likeness.
2) **God's love is eternal and they cannot be separated from it.** Psalm 136:1 declares that "God's love endures forever." Romans 8: 38-39 says— "that nothing can separate us from the love of God in Christ Jesus our Lord." God's love will last always and we can never be separated from it.
3) **God genuinely cares about every detail of their lives.** 1 Peter 5:7 encourages them to—"cast all of their cares on God because He cares for them." God cares about every area of their lives—the good, bad, ugly and indifferent. God cares about them completely. The very hairs on their heads are numbered. God's care goes beyond their ability to care for themselves.
4) **God created them with a purpose.** We find these words in Ephesians 2:10—"We are God's masterpiece, created in Christ Jesus to do good works which God prepared in advance for us to do." God has created our youth on purpose with a purpose, which gives them a reason to put their identity in Him. A long time ago, before the world was formed, God had each of your students in mind. Psalm 139 highlights—"O Lord, you have searched me and you know me...where can I go from your Spirit? Where can I flee from your presence? For you created my inmost being; you knit me together in my mother's womb. I praise you because I am fearfully and wonderfully made. All the days ordained for me were written in your book before one of them came to be."[23]
5) **Identity in Christ is solely based on Christ and His love for us.** Jeremiah 31:3 says—"I have loved you with an everlasting love." Christ loves your young people so much that we find these words to affirm that. Isaiah 46:6 reminds us that, "I (God) have written your name on the palms of my hands."

## Real Talk

There are 5 important things that you can do to help Black youth find their identity in Christ.

1) **Pray for discernment and insight.** Ask the Holy Spirit to show you those students who are struggling with issues of identity. Every student is different, so we need the help of the Holy Spirit to guide us as we lead, encourage, challenge, inspire and mentor young people.
2) **Teach on identity.** Speak/teach on topics that open the way for transformation and offer an invitation for youth to come to Christ in prayer, repentance or petition. Introduce them to Bible verses that speak of their identity in Christ. Guide them into a new way of seeing and believing.
3) **Be transparent about your own identity crisis.** Every Christian has struggled with identity in Jesus, so be open to sharing yours. We serve and encourage others from a place of weakness rather than strength. Be honest about your struggle, I know someone in the group will find a connection with you.
4) **Give youth the opportunity to share their struggles with the youth group.** Hearing the struggles of their peers changes the game for young people. Youth no longer feel like they are the only one going through a difficult time.
5) **Educate parents.** Reaching out to parents who affect the identity of your youth the most is important. Parents are still the number one influencers in their child's life, so it's important to support them in grounding their children in the truth of who God created them to be.

## The Blessing of a Christ Centered Identity

Helping Black youth find their identity in Christ does four things: provides stability, self-worth, purpose and confidence. No matter what happens in life, God does not change the way He sees or feels about them. By finding their identity in Christ, Black youth experience stability because God remains the same. When everything around them is in transition, God is there and he does not change. When Black youth internalize the reality that the God of the universe, creator of everyone and everything, created them in His image it offers permanence. Having a God who cares about the intricate details of their lives shows them that they have immeasurable worth. Placing their identity in Christ gives them a future with hope. God has a purpose and plan for every life he creates. Their purpose is in Christ and by strengthening that relationship, their purpose becomes clearer. There is confidence in knowing that God is an unshakeable and unstoppable presence that deeply cares for them.

We must make our students aware of and understand that the devil is seeking to steal, kill and destroy their identity. He consistently and steadily prowls around seeking who he might devour.[24] Satan would love for Black youth to choose anything other than Jesus for their sense of self. They must be reminded that situations and circumstances do not have to dictate their identity. Their identity can be stable if it is completely grounded in God, who created them and gives them hope. Forming a Christ centered identity leads the way for Black youth to discover who and whose they are.

## Chapter Two

# Hope—Black Youth and Black History

*"A people without knowledge of their past history, origin and culture is like a tree without roots."*[25]

During my tenure as a pastor in a rural church in Virginia, I was blessed with the opportunity to build many relationships. However, some of the most meaningful connections I experienced were with the youth of the congregation. On one particular occasion, one of the teenagers stopped in my office before youth choir rehearsal and asked, "Ms. Richelle, why do we have to celebrate Black History month? Why can't we have a multicultural history month and everybody celebrate together?" Honestly, I wasn't expecting that question, so I did not know how to respond. As is typical for me, I answered her question with a question. "What's wrong with celebrating 'your' history and 'your' culture?" She replied, "There's nothing wrong with it, but all we do is learn about the same people—Martin Luther King, Jr., Harriet Tubman and Rosa Parks." This fifteen year old teen was absolutely right. Black History month celebrations had been limited to learning about a few historical Black leaders.

Besides learning about the faithful few Black history greats, I've heard other arguments as to why Black youth hate or don't appreciate Black History. Donna Bassette, author of *The Dawson Twins by Way of Egypt—Tales of the Ancestor's Voices* relates a story of her children not being able to relate to African American historical figures primarily because of the way they looked.[26] She asserts that since Black history books read like dictionaries and have poor illustrations, her children are not interested in the material. Bassette continued by comparing her children's Black history research projects to their President's Day research projects. The Black history projects were described as boring and dull, whereas the President's Day projects were interesting and exciting. Bassette cites the opportunity for children to see historical figures as children growing up appealing and motivating rather than encountering them as adults with somber and serious looks. This led her to write a book on Black history that reviewers have described as exciting, full of drama and educational.

The study of a few historical figures and the lack of relational engagement with those figures are significant reasons why some Black youth do not place importance on the study of African American history. However, the media, particularly Hip-Hop culture's depictions of Black history makers, contributes to Black youth's negative attitudes toward the knowledge of their history. In recent years, Hip-Hop personalities have decided to refer to Black History trailblazers in derogatory, denigrating and disrespectful ways. For example, female rap artist Nicki Minaj superimposed a photo of Civil Rights and Black Muslim leader Malcolm X, looking out of a window of his home with a rifle in hand on the cover of Minaj's popular song, "Lookin-Ass Nigga." The truth the photo conveys is that Malcolm X was trying to defend his wife and children from firebombs while under federal surveillance.[27] Minaj's song attacks the reputation of Black men and repeats the N-word forty-two times. After coming under fire from Malcolm X's family and community leaders, Minaj issued an apology.

Following in the same vein, rapper Lil' Wayne recorded a verse using the name of Emmett Till, a fourteen year old Black boy who was murdered in 1955 in Mississippi after supposedly whistling at a white woman. He was beaten, shot and thrown in the river with a cotton gin tied around his neck. [28] The rapper was scrutinized over the lyrics in his song "Karate Chop." Wayne raps, "Beat that pussy up like Emmett Till," using Till's name as a sexual metaphor that compared the beating of Till to rough sex.[29] Amid controversy about the distasteful and offensive lyrics, Lil' Wayne issued an official apology. Hip-Hop mogul Russell Simmons posted a parody title "Harriet Tubman Sex Tape," on his YouTube channel—All Def Digital. The video depicts the iconic former slave and freedom fighter secretly recording her sexual relations with her "Massa" in an attempt to blackmail him.[30] A Change.org petition prompted critics to demand an apology. Simmons apologized and removed the video.

In each of these instances, the Hip-Hop icons were held accountable for their offensive actions and reprimanded for their disregard for African American history. In my estimation, their apologies serve as Band-Aids that cover wounds that have been inflicted as a result of foolish actions. I would revise Marcus Garvey's quote from the beginning of the chapter as a response to Minaj's, Wayne's and Simmons' inappropriate behavior. "People without a correct and proper knowledge and understanding of the sacrifices of their ancestors are like trees without roots." In short, they lack wisdom or the ability to make sound choices and good decisions.

The goal of the "Repertory with Roots" model is Christian wisdom formation, which I define as a process of discipleship that equips youth with an awareness and understanding of who and whose they are. If Christian ministries are not careful, the insufficient modeling and irrelevant ways of engaging youth in African American history celebrations could foster apathetic attitudes about Black history and heritage. This teaching and learning model embraces creativity, critical thinking, transformation and fun through the lens of Black history, Black culture, Black music and the Bible.

The call is to be proactive amidst this reality. A new perspective that begins with understanding why Black history celebrations are a part of the lives of African Americans is needed. In 1933, Dr. Carter G. Woodson, the father of Black history, wrote *The Miseducation of the Negro*. His premise was that neglecting the history of African Americans and distorting the realities of their history in most history books deprived the Black child and his race of a heritage, and reduced him to being considered nothing and nobody. Both this quote and Garvey's quote speak to the cause and effect of a life that disregards the necessity and importance of one's history. "Repertory with Roots" places the transmission of Black history in high esteem. Each lesson in the model incorporates Black history through readings, activities and exercises. The lessons are taught from a past-present-future perspective. Integral to this repertoire is fleshing out what it means to be Black in America, which includes honoring Black American's history considering the present day realities and exploring future possibilities.

Honoring the past begins with Africa. African ancestors were integral to mapping, building and calculating the pyramids, sphinx and obelisks (structures similar to the Washington monuments)[31]. African people also created some of history's greatest civilizations. This African past must be taught, embraced and viewed as a legacy worth emulating by the Black youth of today. "Sankofa" is an African word from the Akan tribe in Ghana. It translates as "return and fetch it." It is a symbol that emphasizes the importance of learning from the past, which ensures a strong future.[32] The Akan people believe, and I agree that Black people must move forward and learn new things. In the process of learning and progressing we must not forget the knowledge of the past—Black history. Black youth cite current day celebrations of Black History as exclusive rather than inclusive. As a result, their interest is declining and they question its purpose. This is where youth advocacy becomes necessary. Introducing African history and then following up with African American history, youth advocates teach, support and persuade Black youth to engage our history from the perspectives of future Black history makers. By examining the present state of Black life, followed by envisioning where we go from here, a past-present-future framework can be constructed. Remembering the struggles of African American ancestors and how they overcame the horrors of slavery, Jim Crow, segregation and discrimination to build a better world should motivate and encourage us to think about how to create a better tomorrow for generations not yet born. Youth advocates must help and encourage youth to think in this way.

To demonstrate this past-present-future ideology, consider this brief conversation among high school youth and their teacher at a youth group gathering:

"Someone read the first quote in the box," Mr. Hayes requested.

Jerri raised his hand and offered, "I'll read. 'The Atlantic Slave Trade between the 1500's and the 1800's brought millions of workers from Africa to the southern United States to work on agricultural plantations.'"[33]

Mr. Hayes followed up, "What do you notice about this statement?"

Karen blurted out, "We did not come here as workers; we were forced to come here as slaves. That's a lie."

"Other observations?"

Sharon said, "The caption says 'Patterns of Immigration.' Immigration means people come to a place voluntarily to have a better life or better opportunities. We didn't want to come here from Africa. They brought us here."

Mr. Hayes clarified what had been said. "Black people were brought to America as slaves. Blacks didn't come here because they wanted to."

Mr. Hayes added, "The 2014 textbook that Jerri read from doesn't mention slavery. It doesn't mention the Middle Passage."

"What is the Middle Passage?" David asked.

Mr. Hayes passes out a handout about the Middle Passage and slavery, and asked them to highlight what stood out to them. Highlighted information included:

- Africans were traded as cargo for items such as rum, cloth, guns.
- Human cargo was traded across the Atlantic Ocean.
- Africans often had to lie in each other's feces, urine, or blood.
- The crossing usually took 60-90 days, but it could take up to 4 months.
- 1-2 million died in the crossing.
- Africans were sold in the New World as slaves.
- Slaves were treated as cattle.
- Slaves were bought to work crops[34]

"Mr. Hayes can I ask a question?" Karen requested. "How come the textbook lied about our history?"

"May I ask you a question?" Mr. Hayes asked Karen. "Why do you think they told our history from their point of view?"

Karen shot back, "Because they don't want everyone to know the truth."

"They're probably ashamed of what they did," Jerri chimed in.

"This makes me so mad, I could scream," Sharon said.

"Why don't we learn about the middle passage at school?"

The students continued to ask questions about the textbook and immigration.

"It's 2015 and no one wants to take responsibility for what really happened to my people. Am I supposed to forget about it? Act like it never happened?" Karen wanted to know.

"Our lives mean more than slavery." Mr. Hayes interjected. "Life for Black people began before the Middle Passage. Africa was home to great civilizations like Ancient Egypt. Kings and Queens ruled over the kingdoms of Mali, Songhai and Ghana. African scholars invented calculus, trigonometry and geometry. All this was taking place before the slave traders came. There is so much more to Black history than what you read in that textbook."

The conversation was so rich that it could have continued for more than an hour. To wrap things up, the students were asked to turn to Romans 12: 2 which reads, "Don't copy the behavior and customs of the world, but let God transform you into a new person by changing the way you think. Then you will learn to know God's will for you which is good and pleasing and perfect" (NLT).

Mr. Hayes asked, what does the verse mean to you? He gave each student the opportunity to speak. They went around the table and shared their responses.

David started it off, "You gotta be different from the people in the world."

"God can change my attitude, and after today, I need it," Karen added.

Jerri spoke up and said, "Don't be a copycat. I don't need to be like everyone else."

"God will show me what he wants me to do with my life," Sharon affirmed.

Karen shared the last word, "I need an extreme mind makeover, cause I'm about to catch a case over this textbook."

To bring the session to a close, Mr. Hayes gave his interpretation of the verse: "You can't change other areas of your life if you don't transform your mind first. He asked one final question: "Whose responsibility is it to teach you Black history?"

Consensus prevailed as one by one the teens answered, "It's my responsibility."

"I can't depend on others to do it. This week they called us workers instead of slaves. Who knows what they'll call us next?" Jerri joked.

"Who'll close in prayer?" Mr. Hayes asked.

The opportunity to see past history distorted in a current high school text book led to a revelation for the future. The great thing about history is that it is fluid. Past, present and future are connected. Black history is American history and should not be reduced to observances that span a one month period. Black history is American history and should be celebrated by all Americans.

The possibilities for engaging Black youth in educational forums about their history are limitless. Each repertory lesson includes a process of exploring and engaging material from African American historical resources, such as biographies, autobiographies, historical fiction, songs, books, poetry, movie clips, current events, or quotations. The "Repertory with Roots" pedagogy of engagement offers the space for Black youth and their program facilitators to explore identity questions from the perspective of living as an unashamedly Black child of God. The repertoire calls youth to respect their past history, connect to their current reality and, chart a path for the future. The past, present and future are the foundations for hope.[35]

## Chapter Three

# Values—Black Youth and Black Culture

*"Whatever we believe about ourselves and our ability comes true for us."*[36]

Susan L. Taylor, former editor-in-chief of Essence magazine hit the nail on the head. Beliefs are powerful; they become words. Words become actions, and actions become habits. Habits mirror what person's value. Values define people. Values are operant in what people say and how they live. Much can be learned from observing and interacting with people, particularly young people. The following short vignettes give insight into the value systems of several Black youth that I have observed or interacted with.

**Alicia**[37]

"Alicia, I can't believe you quit another job," Ms. Phillips said to her 19 year-old daughter.

"Mom, you just don't understand. I didn't like the last two jobs, so I applied for this holiday position as a sales associate. You know I love fashion," Alicia countered.

"Fashion has nothing to do with your decision to quit four jobs over the last12 months. Do you know how many people are looking for jobs and can't find them? And you decide to quit every job you get. I don't understand it. What's going to happen when the holiday is over?"

"I'll find another job, I guess," Alicia reluctantly answered. "I'm trying to find something I really want to do. Until I figure out what that is I'll work, I'll quit, I'll get another job."

**Shawna**

"Shawna, you did it!" Her dad exclaimed.

"Thanks Daddy. You always believed in me when no one else did. Everyone said I would get pregnant and drop out of high school but I didn't. Now it's time to move on."

After her graduation dinner, Shawna drove home and packed her bags. She was 18, a high school graduate, and "grown." She decided it was time to move out of her parent's home, move in with her boyfriend, and live at his mother's house. The idea of live-in sex excited Shawna, and she began to pack her things even faster. As she thought about her "boo-thang," she already decided what she was going to wear for their first night of intimacy as an official couple living under the same roof.

### Donna

Donna was angry with her parents and hadn't left her room for the past 24 hours. She realized that being mad at them would not benefit her because her birthday was only three days away. She usually gave her mother a list of things that she wanted. However, this year, there was only one thing she wanted—a car. As Donna looked around her bedroom, she realized that it was filled with everything she could ever need or want—50" flat screen TV, Blu-ray DVD player, Beats By Dr. Dre Pill Speaker, MacBook Air, Wireless printer, king sized bedroom set including a dresser/vanity/mirror set, desk, chair, lamp. Her closet was much too small for all of her designer clothes. Donna said to herself, "Maybe I should ask for a microwave and a small refrigerator, and then I won't have to leave my room." She sighed and wondered why her parents didn't seem to understand and would deprive her of something so important to her—a car.

These stories and others that are similar might be more common than uncommon among today's Black youth. These vignettes represent the work ethic, ideas about sex and materialism. These three stories are evidence that the teaching of values and value centered education must take place in our families, homes, churches, schools, workplaces and communities. What values should be taught? For Black youth, I propose the Nguzo Saba (N-goo-zo Sa-bah) also known as the seven principles of Kwanzaa.

Kwanzaa is an African American holiday which, connects African traditions with American customs, and is celebrated from December 26 through January 1.[38] It was first celebrated by Dr. Maulana Karenga in 1966. The seven core principles are unity, self-determination, collective work and responsibility, cooperative economics, purpose, creativity and faith. Kwanzaa honors the tribal values and traditions that entered America with the kidnapped African men, women and children who were forced to build a life in a strange and hostile land. These ancestors embodied the seven core principles to find a deeper purpose in life.

The principles of Kwanzaa should not only be celebrated the last week in December but all year long. The values of the ancestors offer guidance to Black youth as they journey through today's media saturated culture. The relationship between external forces and values development demonstrate the necessity of reordering the value systems of today's Black youth.

Print and electronic media advertisements play a significant role in the development of values. Youth are bombarded with images every time they surf the internet, watch television or browse through a magazine. Media seems to heavily promote two things—sex and materialism. Ads are creatively crafted to influence young people to engage in sexual activity by making sex seem alluring through purchasing a variety of products; a person cannot even purchase a pack of gum without it being linked to sexual activity.[39]

In addition, materialism also attracts youth to buy into the mindset of covetousness. This desire to have more and more and more stuff continues to grow. According to the article, "Today's Teens More Materialistic, Lessing Willing to Work," compared to previous generations, recent high school students are more likely to want lots of money and nice things, but less likely to say that they are willing to earn them.[40] Young people are admitting that they do not want to work hard, but feel as though they deserve to have whatever they want.

Exposure to advertising plays a major role in youth's materialistic attitudes. Knowing this, it is important to limit exposure to advertising and teach youth to discern media advertising techniques.[41] Helping youth to identify how media messages are contrived and falsified as well as engage them in discerning media techniques will teach youth that media gives false messages. The onslaught of media messages about sex and materialism affect youth's consumer choices and actions.

The seven principles of Kwanzaa describe a value system that can lay a foundation for Black youth values development which counters media messages and reaffirms a commitment to a healthier tomorrow. Through an intentional embrace and implementation of Black values that are lived out daily, Black youth are preparing for the future. Intergenerational networks play a key role in purposeful transmission of values and wisdom. Following a brief description of each of the seven principles a practical strategy to develop value and character will be highlighted.

## Unity

The first core principle is unity. Dr. Karenga defines unity as striving for and maintaining unity in the family, community, nation and race.[42] Unity is the foundational principle. It is a principle and practice of togetherness. It does not simply mean being together; it implies harmonious relationships or oneness.[43] Unity also implies having peace with oneself and one's relationships. The primary value that holds life together is being one with God, the creator. All of life is created by God. It is in God that the creation lives, moves and has their being—Acts 17:28. From God, with God and through God all things are connected.

## Practical Strategy for Exploring Unity

Consider working with an intergenerational group to explore the meaning of unity through African proverbs. A proverb is a wise saying that expresses a truth of some kind. The proverbs found below originated on the continent of Africa by the ancestors.

Each proverb highlights the concept of unity and comes from various African countries or people, which is listed after the proverb. Have a conversation with your group. Discuss the following three questions: What is the proverb saying? What does the proverb mean? How can I apply the proverb to my life?

- To be united is to be strong—Africa
- Teeth without gaps, chew the meat—Buganda
- When spiders unite they can tie up a lion—Ethiopia
- The roof shelters the whole family—Hausa
- We join together to make wise decisions, not foolish ones—Yoruba[44]

After discussing the proverbs, try illustrating them. Allow each participant to share what the proverb means to them and how they are going to live it out.

**Self-Determination**

The second core principle is self-determination. It means to define ourselves, name ourselves, create for ourselves and speak for ourselves.[45] Self-determination is both a commitment and a practice. It requires that African American people define, defend and develop themselves rather than allowing or encouraging others to do it.[46] In addition, self-determination is having a purpose and working toward achieving it without allowing the negative words and actions of others to mislead them. It calls for African Americans to claim their identity both personally and collectively. Dr. Karenga identifies three questions that Black persons should ask themselves about their identities: Who am I? Am I really the person I profess to be? Am I living my life to the fullest?[47]

Librarian, school administrator and author Dorothy Winbush Riley asserts that African Americans must design themselves. Each Black person is born in process and should take responsibility for shaping their identity.[48] The destiny of African American people does not rest in who they are, but what they can become. This principle has to be transmitted to Black youth and pursued constantly and responsibly. To be self-determined is to be free, to live according to the purpose that you have been created for and to leave the world better than you found it.

**Practical Strategy for Exploring Self-Determination**

Being self-determined motivates people to make changes in their lives. Life change occurs during and following deep periods of reflection and probing. People must accept what they find and take responsibility for it so that growth can begin. Real change occurs when the mind accepts the reality that a new way is desirable and possible.

A way to approach self-determination may be through poetry. Using the poem, "Still I Rise," by Maya Angelou as a starting point, ask the following questions: What is the poem's message? What do you learn about self-determination? How can this poem help you on the journey toward self-determination? Ask each young person in your group to write a creative piece (poem, spoken word, song, rap, essay, etc.) entitled "I Can Rise Too." Each person should write in the context of "before and after," identifying what life like was before their change, what life is like now, and what they are expecting to happen in the future. After youth have time to write, give participants the opportunity to share.

### Collective Work and Responsibility

The third core principle is collective work and responsibility. It can be defined as building and maintaining our community together and making our brothers' and sisters' problems our problems and solving them together.[49] This principle highlights African American's collective work, collective identity and collective future. It states that African Americans are collectively responsible for the failures and setbacks as well as victories and achievements of Black people.[50] Embodying collective work and responsibility demonstrates a return to the traditional values of kindness, generosity, patience, tolerance, cooperation and responsibility.[51] This principle demonstrates a way of rebuilding the Black community through serving and working together.

### Practical Strategy for Exploring Collective Work and Responsibility

One option for exploring collective work and responsibility is an activity called Dream a Big Dream. This idea begins with the question: What would you do for the world if you were not afraid? Ask this question to each participant in the group. Pass out markers, pens, pencils and paper to everyone. Give them the opportunity to brainstorm about, draw or map-out their Big Dream. Give each participant the opportunity to share their ideas. Ask the following questions before concluding the activity: How does your big dream include others working together? How does your dream improve the community/world? What daily steps can you take to make your Big Dream come true?

### Cooperative Economics

The fourth core principle is cooperative economics. It means to build and maintain our own stores, shops and other businesses and to profit from them together.[52] Cooperative economics is a commitment to the practice of shared social wealth and working to achieve it. It is the sharing of work and wealth in the context of family. Cooperating economically stresses self-reliance in the building, strengthening and controlling of the economics in the African American community. Generosity to the poor is also stressed as well as finding ways to end their poverty. Ending their poverty can be explored cooperatively through small business opportunities which lead to living sustainable lives.

**Practical Strategy for Exploring Cooperative Economics**

As a group, canvas the community, identifying as many Black owned businesses as you can. Write down the name of the business, the owner and the types of services it offers. Then create a separate list of the most common businesses that Black people support (hair/cosmetics, nails, food, music, clothes, etc.) Canvas the community again. Identify businesses that offer these products. Identify who the owners are. Compare the lists. Ask: What do you notice? What did you learn? What needs to change? Read the following ideas about Black business. Wherever you spend your money is where you create a job opportunity. Spending money in the neighborhood where you live creates a job there. Spending money outside of your neighborhood creates a job in that community. If the businesses you support are not Black owned, at the end of the day, your money goes with them to their community.[53] Lead a discussion with the group and brainstorm ways to build businesses in the Black community.

**Purpose**

The fifth core principle is purpose. Dr. Karenga defines purpose as being committed to the collective calling of building, improving and protecting our community's culture and history. This includes restoring the historical greatness of African American people and contributing to the good and beauty in the world.[54]

Knowing who we are as African Americans, and where we are going demonstrates that there is purpose for our lives. Part of that purpose is preserving and increasing the legacy that the ancestors left us. God the creator gives each of us a purpose; when we live within that pathway to purpose, our passions and life becomes full of promise, pride and progress. When we realize that our purpose is ordained by God, nothing can stop us from moving forward. The foundational component of purpose is living a life of service and seeking to make the world a better place. Service connects us to our purpose because it provides the opportunity to live out Christ's great command of loving God, loving our neighbor and loving ourselves.

**Practical Strategy for Exploring Purpose**

Choose a population (children, youth, adults, seniors, homeless, etc.) who your group feels called to serve. You might consider dividing a large group into smaller groups to serve more than one population. Set up a service activity by contacting an agency that serves your population; ask what types of assistance they could use. After you set up the logistics, obtain parental permission, coordinate transportation, lead the youth in acts of service. Following your trip, debrief the experience. Ask the following questions or others like them:

- Will someone describe the project we completed?
- What did you notice or learn at the site?
- Did any of these things surprise you?
- What do you know now that you didn't know before?
- What attitudes and feelings do you have about the experience that you didn't have before?
- What part of the project was most valuable for you?
- What are some things that would have made the group experience better for you?
- What changes would you suggest for future group experiences?
- Where does the group go from here?

## Creativity

The sixth core principle is creativity. It means to do always as much as we can, in the way that we can, in order to leave our community more beautiful and beneficial than we inherited it.[55] This principle focuses on how African Americans can use their talents, imagination and creative skills to bring beauty and restoration to the community. It also means honoring and remembering the ancestors whose legacy we stand on today. Creativity is spiritual, yet manifests itself in the physical. Everyone is creative. It is not just reserved for artists, writers, dancers or inventors. Seeing an ordinary thing in a unique way is using creativity. Creativity is using the never-ending gift of imagination to leave the world a better place.

## Practical Strategy for Exploring Creativity

To explore creativity, you can establish a creativity corner. Fill the space with craft supplies such as markers, paints, modeling clay, colored paper, beads, string and yarn. Invite students to use this space to create anything they want with the materials provided. Play some soft music in the background. At the end of the activity, give the participants the opportunity to share their creations. Ask each participant: What inspired you to create this work of art?

## Faith

The seventh core principle is faith. It can be defined as believing with all our heart in our people, our parents, our teachers, our leaders and the righteousness and victory of our struggle.[56] For the Christian believer, faith begins with belief in the triune God, followed by faith in oneself and others. Faith inspires African Americans to transcend and transform difficulties with thoughtful action.[57] To grow in faith, one must be mindful of their thoughts, words and beliefs; they must not allow the negative to encircle their mind and move in. Proponents of faith believe in hope. African Americans recall their cultural and historical past in an effort to focus on the story of the future. African Americans should work together, believing, hoping for and working toward building stronger communities that promote harmony, beauty, justice, truth and prosperity.

**Practical Strategy for Exploring Faith**

Motown Diva Diana Ross said, "The more you believe in yourself, the more you can develop an internal power source, out of which comes the strength to choose a positive outlook on life."[58] World renowned educator and advisor to United States presidents, Dr. Mary McLeod Bethune said in her "Last Will and Testament," "Without faith, nothing is possible; with it nothing is impossible. Faith in God is the greatest power, but great too is faith in oneself."[59] Share these quotes with your group, and ask the following questions:

- How are the quotes connected?
- What can we learn from them?
- How can you apply them to your life?
- What difference do these quotes make?

After discussion, invite participants to write down prayer requests, thoughts or ideas that are challenging their faith. Put those slips of paper in a box. Sit the box in the center of the room. Gather in a circle around the box and offer a prayer for strength, courage and increased faith.

The seven principles of Kwanzaa offer a framework for the transmission and cultivation of African centered values and character traits for Black youth. This chapter has described the deteriorating value systems of today's Black youth, and introduced the seven principles of Kwanzaa as a method of exploring an idea of sharing practical strategies for valued centered education. By combatting negative and pervasive media images, there is hope for encouraging Black youth to pay homage to Black ancestors and continue their legacy of making the world a better place.

## Chapter Four

# Our Song—Black Youth and Black Music

*"Party people, party people can y'all get funky...Rock, rock to the Planet Rock, don't stop...We gotta rock it don't stop it, we gotta rock it don't stop..."*[60]

"That's my song!" I yelled to my friends every time I heard the 1982 Hip-Hop hit "Planet Rock" by Afrika Bambaataa and the Soulsonic Force. As a teenager coming of age in suburban Philadelphia, Pennsylvania, I would gather in our neighborhood playground to hang out, talk, and listen to the sounds of Luther Vandross, Rick James, Teena Marie, Grandmaster Flash and the Furious Five, Michael Jackson and so many others. To our crew, Black music was an expression of what we were experiencing during our tumultuous teen years. The phrase "That's my song!" was used by everyone in the group as we engaged Black Music on a personal and emotional level. Shouting it while the music played indicated that the person shouting had an extremely personal connection to the song—the beat, words or feeling. Shouting it out was sometimes prompted by how the artists looked; some of my girlfriends expanded the phrase, saying, "That's my song, and that's my baby singing it. You know he's singing to me, right?" Each of us declared our territorial affiliations with specific artists and songs; the reality was that it was "our song."

As a community of friends, we embraced Black music and found strength, hope and inspiration in it. We learned about pertinent issues in urban communities through the political commentary of rap artists. We thought about love and what it might look like in our lives as we listened to the smooth sounds of R&B. We tried the latest dance moves as we moved soulfully to the pop hits of the day. Our song, Black music, I dare say, is to the youth of today what it was to me during my teen years. It continues to be the same today—a transcendent conversation partner that informs my spiritual story.

Earlier I mentioned "Planet Rock," a feel good Hip-Hop track that blends synthesizers, voice encoders and breakbeats. This song was extremely instrumental in my decision to try break dancing as a hobby.

This is a part of my spiritual story that most people do not know about. All of the break dancers in my neighborhood were male. All of the break dancers in the surrounding communities were male. All of the break dancers that I saw on TV were male. There were no female break dancers. Something was wrong with that. I needed to be the one to do something about that. I needed to break into the male dominated break dancing community in suburban Philadelphia. My family had always taught me that I could do anything I wanted to, if I put my mind to it and worked hard. So, I put my mind to it, asked my male break dancing friends to help me and worked hard. I didn't know if my friends secretly wanted me to fail or thought that I was a serious contender in breakdancing. Whatever their intentions were, they proved themselves to be good teachers and encouraged me to test my skills in front of a group during a dance competition. I competed but did not win, but I continued to compete. I did not give up.

In retrospect, "Planet Rock" was my motivator to try and not give up. Every morning before going to work at summer camp, I would listen to, sing along with and dance to the song. If it were not for "Planet Rock," I may not have ventured out to try breakdancing. The infectious beat, the simple lyrics contained a message, "Rock and don't stop it, rock and don't stop." In other words, don't give up. Persevere, never give up! "Planet Rock," doesn't include philosophically deep lyrics but a message that I have remembered and applied thirty years later. Persevere, never give up. Black music is embraced by many ethnic groups; vocalists of all cultures seek to replicate its sound. Black music is our song.

## Black Music: Genres and Subgenres

Black music is not limited to America. Its evolution has been and continues to be a worldwide phenomenon. We pay homage to its roots on the African continent. As a result of the transatlantic slave trade, Africans were transported all over the world. The music moved with them. The purpose of African music has been conveyed by Cameroonian artist, musician and writer Frances Bebey who says, The purpose of African music is to translate daily experiences into living sound, to portraying life, nature or the supernatural.[61]

For more than 400 years, this intention has been consistently connected to the creative development of Black music genres and subgenres throughout the trajectory of Black musical history. Following is a list of the genres and outlined in *The Encyclopedia of African American Music—Volume Three—P-Z—* Spirituals, Ragtime, Blues, Gospel, Jazz, Rap and Hip-Hop.[62] Subgenres are also identified in the encyclopedia. Volume Three provides a detailed summary of Black music.

Music is one of the deepest and most holistic forms of human communication. It speaks to us physically, emotionally, intellectually and spiritually in ways that touch us deeply. Black music is a means of self-expression, offers political commentary, and provides inspiration; it constructs positive meaning in the lives of people who engage it. Black music forms the individual and communal identity of Black youth.

## Black Music—Linking the Generations

Theologians and Musicians Don and Emily Saliers assert that since time began communities have explored their identity and destiny through music. The Saliers use the term "songlines" to refer to music that links the generations.[63] From generation to generation people are connected through songlines. In African American history and culture, the songline began in the villages in Africa. Through call and response it developed in the Americas with the creation of spirituals. It continued to undergo expansion with the advent of ragtime, blues, gospel, jazz, rap and hip-hop. Black music uses the hardships, trials, experiences and triumphs of life in creating music that strengthens, inspires and brings hope. According to the Saliers, music recreates our worldview and we exist within that worldview in the midst of fear, beauty, pain and the pleasures of existence.[64] Music expresses and shapes emotions, and strong emotional connections with music emerge when one listens carefully. We take ownership of the music when we bring something of ourselves to both the creating and listening acts. Music makes meaning when we listen attentively. We must develop a "soul for hearing" that will allow us to hear the soul of the music.[65] Hearing the soul or the depth of the music helps us to connect with the rhythm as well as the lyrics.

The composition, lyrics and sound of Black music allow its listeners to develop a "soul for hearing" through the lyrics; listeners can feel and hear the soul of the music. Listeners move beyond beats and rhythms to hear the inner voice of the artist, and through the vocalist's story, listeners formulate ideas about their own identity in positive and negative terms. Music is a strong and positive force in helping youth in discovering who they are and who they may become. Black music gives youth an aesthetic medium to explore identity and voice amidst what is often the chaos of daily living. Within that method they may encounter biblical and theological themes that support Christian discipleship.

## Black Music as Realized Hope

Black music affirms a realized hope in the lives of Black youth. Hope is affirmed and a present reality. Theologically, Black youth find hope in the present day-to-day circumstances in which they find themselves, and realizing that things can and will get better. By no means am I suggesting that all examples of Black music are hope-filled; in fact quite the contrary, Black music is flawed. However, what I am suggesting is that through engaging in wise listening and critical reflection, youth are given the tools to discern and grapple with the hard issues that Black lyrical content presents. Engaging in theological wrestling offers opportunities for making positive meaning.

The following is an exploration of three lyrical compositions that offer theological evidence of hope. The songs are "I am Not My Hair" by India. Arie, "Don't Shoot" by the Game and "Lovin' Me" by the R & B Divas. Each composition offers lyrical content that is rich in delineating societal issues confronted by today's Black youth. A basic theological framework that can be employed when engaging lyrical texts include—listening, linking, looking, and leading. First, one should listen critically or listen with a purpose. Second, after listening one should make a link or make connections between what was heard and his or her own life. After linking, one should look for the big picture of how God is speaking through theological or biblical themes that are incorporated into the song's message. Finally, one should ask where this song leading me? How will thoughts, words and deeds change as a result of theological engagement?

## I AM NOT MY HAIR

India. Arie, Grammy award winning singer, songwriter, musician and record producer who sings soul, neo-soul and folk music, sings "I Am Not My Hair." This song describes India's journey of wearing a press and curl, Jheri curl, relaxer, dreadlocks and afro. After a time of self-reflection, India declared, "I am not my hair," indicating her refusal to be defined by her hair. Verse two says:

Good hair means curls and waves; bad hair means you look like a slave
At the turn of the century, it's time for us to redefine who we be,
You can shave it off like a South African beauty
Or get in lock like Bob Marley
You can rock it straight like Oprah Winfrey
If it's not what's on your head, it's what's underneath say hey...I am not my hair[66]

To enter into a time of theological reflection using the listen, link, look and lead framework, the following questions might be considered:

1. Listen: What is India saying? What is her message?
2. Link: What types of hairstyles do you prefer? Why?
3. Look: What do you think God's thoughts are about Black hair? What makes you say this? How does your answer reveal what you think about Black hair? Read 1 Peter 3: 3-4. Does what you read match what you said previously?
4. Lead: What is one new idea that you can apply to your life and your perception of Black hair?

These questions help youth to enter a space where they are called to confront ideologies and stereotypes and enter into a conversation about Black hair, which is a serious and oftentimes detrimental topic of contention in the Black community. The lyrics provide a constructive example of empowerment by challenging Black youth to embrace who they are based on inner beauty rather than outer beauty. Appendix E—A Hair Journey will offer a more detailed experiential teaching and learning session on the historical and contemporary meanings of good and bad hair.

## DON'T SHOOT

Rapper, The Game collaborated with a team of Hip-Hop artists to produce a track entitled, "Don't Shoot" which brings attention to the murder of Michael Brown in Ferguson, Missouri in 2014. The song places Michael Brown in a lineage that includes Emmett Till, Trayvon Martin and others who have been murdered unjustly. Acts of violence against unarmed Black men have been at the forefront of media news coverage for several years. It is a problem that parents of young Black men fear. Verse two and the hook share the essence of the song's message:

Yo, come on we gotta stick together, we all we got
Police taking shots and I ain't talking 'bout Ciroc
I'm talking bout Emmett Till, I'm talking about Ezell Ford
I'm talking bout Sean Bell, they never go to jail for
Trayvon over Skittles, Mike Brown Cigarillos
History keeps repeating itself, like a Biggie instrumental
America's a glass house and my revenge is mental
Rather use my brain than throw a cocktail through a window
Time to take a stand and save our future
Like we all got shot, we all got shot
Throwing up our hands don't let them shoot us
Cause we all we got, we all we got
God ain't put us on the Earth to get murdered, its murder
God ain't put us on the Earth to get murdered, its murder
Don't point your weapons at me.[67]

Critical reflection on the following questions can help listeners to make meaning of the message.

1. Listen: Who is this song about? What has happened?
2. Link: As a black youth growing up in America, what are some of your challenges? On a scale from 1- 10 rate your top ten challenges and why.
3. Look: Where is God when we hear of unarmed Black men being shot by police officers? Does God care?
4. Lead: The hook says, "God ain't put us on the earth to get murdered, its murder." What did God put us on earth for? Read Mark 12: 29-31. What is your purpose?

These questions assist youth in thinking through ways to deal with injustice. An experiential teaching on this theme will be presented in Appendix B—Life Matters.

**LOVIN' ME:**

"Lovin' Me" is an upbeat motivational track on the compilation album R & B Divas led by recording artist Faith Evans. R & B Singers Nicci Gilbert, Monifah, Syleena Johnson and Keke Wyatt come together to lend their voices in an anthem of empowerment that addresses the issues of body image and self-esteem among Black women. The lyrics speak powerfully and passionately:

It's been a long time...yeah, since I looked in the mirror...and liked what I see
It was a hard climb...yeah, things are much clearer in my reality and how people see me
Always feeling ashamed because of what I was told
Now, I'm taking the ugly and make it beautiful, yeah
I found me a place, where I ain't doing nothing,
But lovin' myself and everything about me
Said, I found me a place where it don't even matter,
What nobody else thinks, cause I'm lovin me![68]

Thinking about the lyrics and the reality that Black teens face regarding body image and self-esteem, the following questions might be considered:

1. Listen: If you had to organize this song with a beginning, middle and end, how would you do it?
2. Link: How might the lyrics of this song reflect what you have experienced in your life?
3. Look: Read Genesis 1: 27 how does this inform how you think about yourself and how you look?
4. Lead: How can this song motivate you to see yourself as God sees you?

This example of theological reflection may not solve the problems of low self-esteem or answer all of the questions about body image among Black youth, but they do however, provide a space and place for constructive dialogue.

Black music helps listeners to express themselves. It challenges them to consider the social injustices found in the communities and world. Black music inspires, builds hope, and strengthens listeners during the good and bad of their lives. When there is very little that seems to make sense in the world, hearing the right song whether, gospel, pop, hip-hop or R &B can create great feelings of joy. It helps make meaning out of day to day experiences. The sound may move listeners, but the lyrics compel them to greater heights of awareness and reflection. Black music is a catalyst in helping Black youth answer the questions of who and whose they are. A Zairian proverb says, "The tree cannot stand without its roots."[69] Black music is one of those roots that stand as a source of identity.

## Chapter Five

# Word Up—Black Youth and Bible

*"How can a young person stay pure? By obeying your word."*[70]

One thing I appreciate about reading scripture is that sometimes the biblical text asks a question, and before I have the opportunity to engage in serious thought, the answer shows up in the next verse or surrounding verses. Psalm 119:9 is an example; it gives the answer on how to prevent sin in our lives. In a straightforward manner, the psalmist replies that—we avoid sin by living according to God's word. Studying the word of God should be a lifelong endeavor. One cannot live according to God's word without being personally acquainted with it. The Bible provides resources for resolving life's dilemmas, making the right decisions and distinguishing true values from worldly opinions. Psalm 119:9 teaches how to live as children of God. The Bible is needed as a guide in the Christian's life journey.

Throughout the years that I have served in ministry, teaching the Bible to Black youth has been one of my favorite ministry responsibilities. Beginning with my tenure as a youth minister and Rites of Passage Director in Baltimore City, Maryland; through my sojourn as an associate minister and pastor in rural King and Queen, Virginia, and now as a college professor and associate minister in Grand Rapids, Michigan, I have loved spending time engaging the scriptures with Black youth.

Below is a conversation that took place in a recent gathering of middle and high school young ladies who are members of the Daughters of Imani Christian Rites of Passage Ministry. They were participating in Table Talk, which is an informal opportunity for the young sisterhood and their adult mentors to get together and "just talk." A formal, structured lesson is not planned during this time; instead, the group comes together, brings their questions to the table and talk about them. One evening, Brittani came ready to talk.

"There's this boy at my school who is driving me crazy. He says that there is no God. That's fine if that's what he believes, but he doesn't have to challenge my beliefs in class. I believe in God, he believes in whatever."

I asked, "What's the problem? Are you trying to convert him or make him believe in God?"

"No, way! He can believe what he wants. It's just that he tries to embarrass me in front of the class when I won't talk about what I believe, and the teacher doesn't do anything about it. I went to her and told her that she needs to stop him from harassing me and trying to make me look stupid. If he's not religious, that's his choice. But I am religious, and we don't need to talk about it in school."

I was intrigued by Brittani's response. I asked, "So you say you are religious. What does that mean?"

She paused before responding. "I believe. I go to church, you know what I mean?"

I responded, "No, I don't know what you mean. A lot of people believe—Jews, Buddhists, Muslims, Christians. All these people are religious. So what are you? Jewish? Buddhist? Muslim? Christian? What do you believe?"

Brittani sidestepped answering the questions by saying, "I just get so mad when he challenges me, and sometimes I just start crying."

"Why do you cry?" I asked rhetorically. "If you know what you believe, then there shouldn't be a problem. Being a Christian is more than being religious; it's about having a relationship with Jesus Christ. It's more than going to church. It's about spending time with God in prayer and reading the Bible. I want to open this conversation to everyone because I want to hear what everyone is thinking."

Gathered around the table are nine young ladies—eight high school students and one middle school student. I asked the question, "What do you believe?" I was completely shocked that none of them responded. There was complete silence. In my mind I heard crickets chirping. As I visually scanned the room, some looked like deer that were caught in headlights while others just lowered their heads. I was expecting these girls to shout out responses like popcorn popping. But it didn't happen that way. I concluded two things were possible: 1) These young women were simply not sure of what they believed or, 2) They had difficulty articulating what they believe. I also found it interesting that they did not even attempt to articulate what their family members and friends believed.

For example, when I was a child growing up, I would try to claim my grandmother's beliefs as my own. I heard my grandmother speak of Jesus as a friend. So, as I grew up, naturally I believed that Jesus was my friend too. My grandmother sang a hymn that helped to understand who Jesus was. She sang: "Jesus is all the world to me, My life, my joy, my all; He is my strength from day to day, without him I would fall; When I am sad, to Him I go, no other one can cheer me so, When I am sad, he makes me glad. He's my friend".[71] This hymn spoke of the trust and assurance of Jesus and how He relates to us as a companion on life's journey. Because this was my grandmother's faith association, it became mine as well even though I was unable to articulate my own beliefs at that time. Given my experience, I found it interesting that the young ladies did not articulate what they have heard from others. As they sat there unresponsive, my heart became heavy. I thought to myself, how will they navigate the tumultuous waters of adolescence if they are unable to articulate what they believe?

To help them better understand how to identify and articulate what they believe, I referenced the Apostle's Creed, an early statement of the Christian faith. Each Sunday our church family stands together and recites it:

> "I believe in God the Father, Almighty; maker of heaven and earth, and in Jesus Christ his only son our Lord; who was conceived by the Holy Spirit, born of the Virgin Mary, suffered under Pontius Pilate; was crucified, dead and buried; the third day he arose from the dead, ascended into heaven and sits on the right hand of God the father Almighty, from thence He will come to judge the quick and the dead. I believe in the Holy Spirit, the church universal, the communion of saints, the forgiveness of sins, the resurrection of the body, and the life everlasting."[72]

To make the reading of this ancient faith statement come alive, the girls and the leadership team walked through the scriptures and, examined passages that correlated with each faith statement of the creed. Passages on God, creation, Jesus' conception, suffering, crucifixion, death, burial, resurrection, Holy Spirit, the beginning of the Christian church, Holy Communion, forgiveness of sins and eternal life were explored. I think during that moment, the girls began to identify the Bible not just as a collection of irrelevant, disconnected stories, but as a story of how God sent Jesus to save us from sin. The next task is to help them identify their personal story as a part of God's great story. Several believed that the creed was only a statement to be memorized and recited during the worship service. Hopefully, now they view it as a legitimate articulation of what they believe.

Following our trek through the Apostle's Creed and the scriptures, I asked the following questions: How many of you read your Bible? If you don't read it, why not? Answers varied: "I don't make it a priority." "I let other things come first." "I read it when I need to, like when things are going wrong." "I don't always understand what I'm reading." "I don't have time." Keeping this in mind, I wonder: How can we do a better job of helping Black youth engage with the scriptures?

**What is the Bible?**

Oftentimes when this question is asked, the automatic response is "the Bible is the word of God." Hearing a response like this closes possible doors for discussion. By responding with "the word of God," it signals that there is very little left to talk about. It is such a matter of fact answer. Black youth do not need matter of fact answers; they need understanding. More can be shared about the scripture that will generate an interest in the Bible and its purpose.

The Bible is a collection of books written by 40 men covering a period of approximately 1,600 years.[73] It was written by specific people for a specific purpose. The Bible is the greatest story of all time. It is the story of the God of all the living, true in all his ways. He passionately loves his children and has established the way of salvation through Jesus Christ constructing a way for eternity. [74] The Bible is Jesus centered. It is the story of how Jesus was in the beginning with God. He left his royal throne in heaven, became a man and moved into the neighborhood as God in flesh. The Bible is the story of the Holy Spirit, the spirit of truth who existed in the beginning of creation, moved across the face of the waters, and who manifested His presence on the Day of Pentecost, and who abides with us now. God the Father, God the Son, and God the Holy Spirit are alive today. The Bible is more than a collection of stories. The Bible is a living account of God's grace in our lives. It is the story of how God calls each person to write his or her own story in light of God's story. This description of what the Bible is all about will motivate Black youth to want to know more about God's word.

### What Bible Translation Should I Use?

Prior to choosing a translation, it is important to make youth aware that the Bible was originally written in Hebrew, Greek and Aramaic. It is critical to introduce youth to more than one Bible translation because different Bible translations tend toward different interpretation.[75] Some of the most widely read translations include the Message (MSG), the Living Bible (TLB), and the Amplified Bible (AMP). However, they tend to be liberal with paraphrasing, which gives too much room for personal interpretation.[76] Other translations I love to use while studying, teaching or preaching include the New International Version (NIV), New International Reader's Version (NIRV) New Revised Standard Version (NRSV), Today's New International Version (TNIV), New Living Translation (NLT), New Century Version (NCV), and Common English Bible (CEB).

However, before choosing a translation for your young people, I strongly suggest that you do some research. I also encourage you as a youth leader to invest in a study Bible that has foot notes and marginal notes. Study Bibles for youth will also include articles and quotes that inspire application in the reader's life. Choosing more than one translation may prove to be helpful as well because it will allow readers to compare different translations. If you would like to explore various Bible translations without purchasing multiple Bibles, take a look at Bible Gateway (http//:www.biblegateway.com). Only you can decide which translation will work for you and the needs of your group.

### What Difference Does Context Make?

Teaching the Bible in context is vital for students to have a big picture understanding of the Bible.[77] Teaching a passage of scripture without providing the context fails to help them see the "big picture view" of scripture.[78] Teaching in context helps students to grasp the overarching Bible story. When we don't teach the Bible in context, scripture becomes less effective.[79] The Bible becomes a loose collection of unrelated stories and isolated verses.[80] Contextual teaching preserves the thread of the Bible's purpose. Teaching any passage without providing the context, does the youth a disservice because it fails to help them see the big picture view of scripture. Andy Blanks, author of *"The 7 Best Practices of Teaching Teenagers the Bible"* offers three ways to teach the Bible in context. First, one begins teaching the Bible in context by looking for the big picture. The reader should place the book of the Bible that the verse being studied is in into the overall timeline of scripture—Old Testament, New Testament, Prophets, Gospel, Epistles, etc.[81] Second, after situating the passage/verse in its context, one can ask the following three questions: 1) Who wrote the book? 2) When was it written? 3) Why was it written? Finally, the teacher can help the students know where the passage fits into the surrounding text by summarizing. Teaching contextually takes more preparation, but it's worth the effort because it helps young people view the Bible as a story written by God, inspiring people in a certain cultural context with a specific purpose in mind.

## How Do I Study the Bible?

Black youth want to understand the Bible when they read it. Unfortunately, reading the Bible without comprehending it is not helpful when trying to grow in relationship with God. One youth asked, "Why would God write his word in a book that's not easy for people to understand?" This question prompted me to search for a method of studying the Bible that helps readers to understand and apply the words of scripture. In my search, I encountered the inductive method of studying the scriptures. The inductive method empowers readers to engage in personal Bible study. It gives them the opportunity to interact with God's word personally; it encourages them to apply the message of the Bible on their hearts.[82] Inductive Bible study uses the Bible itself as a primary source of information about the Bible.[83] Inductive study draws youth into a personal interaction with scripture. It consists of three phases: observation, interpretation, application.

**Observation** answers the question: What does the passage say?[84] This is the starting point of the study. Observation is discovering what the passage is saying. It takes time and practice. Discovering what the passage says includes answering the who, what, when, where, why and how questions about the passage being studied.

**Interpretation** answers the question: What does the passage mean?[85] The basis for accurate interpretation is careful observation. Interpretation is the process of discovering what the passage means. It flows out of observation. Using cross references, followed by Bible dictionaries, word studies and commentaries can supplement study during the interpretation phase.

**Application** answers the question: How does the meaning of this passage apply to me?[86] Once a person knows what a passage means, he or she is held accountable for putting it into practice for his or her own lives. Following this view, the goal of personal Bible study is a transformed life and a growing relationship with Jesus Christ.[87]

The inductive method is one of many Bible study methods that could be used. However, I have included it because it uses the Bible to interpret the Bible as a method of engaging and exploring the scriptures. The four basic questions in this section—What is the Bible? What Bible translation should I use? What difference does context make? How do I study the Bible?—provide a framework for further engagement and exploration of God's word.

### Ideas for Bible Study Engagement and Exploration

The following suggestions are several strategies for youth to engage and explore the scriptures in meaningful and transformative ways:

### Back to the Basics

Develop a list of faith basics that youth should know by the time they graduate high school. Some faith basics our group identified include: salvation, love, grace, prayer, and faith. To facilitate this process, divide youth into small groups of 3 to 4 youth. Give them the opportunity to agree on the five most important basic truths of the Christian faith. Gather the group together and ask the small groups to report; then challenge the group to synthesize all of the suggestions into a final set of five truths. Compare their list to your own. You might consider inviting the senior pastor to a group meeting to participate.

### Bible Reading[88]

Make Bible reading purposeful and memorable. One of the best ways to read and understand the Bible is to reenact Bible events. Challenge youth to discover how a character acted and felt by stepping into that character's shoes.[89]

*"The Bible Passage as a Script."* Assign each student a role; then guide them in acting it out. Choose passages where everyone can get involved. Following the dramatization, invite the young people who played the various roles to comment on what the character teaches and how to apply that truth to life.

*"Mystery Question"* Give the youth a question where they have to search the scripture to find an answer. Mystery questions let Bible reading become a search for God's answers and listening for God's advice.[90] For example, youth might be challenged to find the fears Moses had about being a leader in Exodus 3:7 – 4:13.

*"Read with Tools"* To encourage young people to read through difficult portions of scripture, show them how to use Bible study tools to discover the answers they are looking for. Bring in a concordance, a

Bible dictionary and a Bible commentary. Show the youth how these resources work. A concordance is a listing of Bible words in alphabetical order with verses that use the word. This tool is helpful for finding Bible verses. A Bible dictionary defines words used in the Bible. A commentary contains insights into the meaning of Bible passages. Ask students to identify times when they could use each tool.[91]

## Bible Biography

To engage students in exploration of the scriptures, select a biblical personality and follow that person's life and faith.[92] Examine their failures and triumphs. You can do a Bible biography in two ways. Ask one person to write a one page summary of the person's life. Provide Bible references to help the youth with their research. The young person will read the scriptures and write a brief biography to be presented to the group at the next meeting. The second way is for the youth leader to prepare the biography and discussion questions, and then selects someone to read it and follow up the reading with discussion.

## Credo

Many churches recite or confess the Apostle's Creed as a statement of belief. A creed can be used to explore the biblical basis of the confession.[93] Invite youth to study the creed line by line referencing the following Bible references in the Apostle's Creed.

- I believe in God the Father Almighty (Genesis 1:1, Philippians 1:2)
- Maker of Heaven and Earth (Genesis 1:1)
- And in Jesus Christ, His only Son our Lord (John 1:18)
- Who was conceived by the Holy Spirit (Luke 1:31, Matthew 1:18)
- Born of the Virgin Mary (Luke 1:34, 2:7)
- Suffered under Pontius Pilate (Mark 15:15)
- Was crucified (Luke 23:33)
- Dead and buried (Luke 23:46, John 19:40-42)
- The third day He rose from the dead (Luke 24:1-2)
- He ascended into heaven (Acts 1:9)
- And sits at the right hand of God the Father Almighty (Mark 14:62)
- From thence He shall come to judge the quick and the dead (Matthew 13:41-43)
- I believe in the Holy Spirit (Acts 1:5, 1 John 3:24)
- The Church Universal (Matthew 16:18, 1 Corinthians 12:12)
- The communion of saints (Hebrews 10:24-25, 12:1)
- The forgiveness of sins (1 John 1:8-9)
- The resurrection of the body (1 Corinthians 15:35-44, 1 Peter 1:3-4)

- And the life everlasting (John 3:16)

## Bible Journal

A journal can be used as a guide to reading the Bible on a regular basis. It might include Bible lessons or topics to be studied, or it may focus on a particular book or section of the Bible. To further promote Bible reading, you might include on each page 2-3 questions based on the scripture for the day. This gives opportunity to reflect on what they are reading. A journal is a great tool to strengthen deeper faith and biblical understanding.[94] These creative ideas connect real life with faith basics and provide Black youth with opportunities to engage and explore the Bible.

## Part One Summary

This unit on Roots and Sources of Identity began with an understanding of the race and spirituality of Black youth. We explored how race and spirituality historically and culturally inform African American youth identity. A survey of Black history and how Black youth respond to African American historical figures was highlighted. Various Hip-Hop personalities were examined for their disrespect for the contributions and legacy of African American trailblazers; these personalities showed a lack of wisdom and sound judgment. In spite of these poor examples, Black youth are encouraged to honor past history, connect it to their present reality and chart a course for becoming America's current history-makers. In addition to appraising Black history, part one also demonstrated how Black culture is undergirded by an African American value system. This classification demonstrates the potential to offer solutions to the breakdown of values in the Black family and community. This scaffolding of values centered on Black culture builds character and hope.

Further exploration took place in the form of exploring Black music which exhibits a positive meaning making function in the lives of Black youth. Black music links the generations and affirms a realized hope in the lives of African American youth. Finally, the poor relationship between Black youth and the Bible was explored. Black youth do not prioritize reading and studying the Bible, and when they do read the scriptures, they do not understand the content. To promote and encourage engagement and exploration of the scriptures four questions were presented. This beginning survey led to further scriptural encounters through practical ideas and strategies for teaching and learning. Part One—Black Youth: Roots and Sources of Identity delineate a framework for a vision for ministry with Black youth. Part Two—The Vision: Relational, Real and Relevant will delineate the foundational vision upon which Repertory with Roots is built. This framework will identify key components for transformative ministry with Black youth.

## Part 2

# The Vision—Relational, Real and Relevant

## Chapter Six

# Visions of Discipleship—Wisdom, African American and Christian Wisdom Formation

*"One of the first things I think young people especially nowadays should learn is how to see for yourself and listen for yourself and think for yourself."*[95]

These prophetic words spoken by Black Nationalist Leader Malcolm X more than fifty years ago, echo the societal and cultural truth that wisdom is in short supply in the lives of young African Americans. Seeing for yourself, listening for yourself and thinking for yourself are the beginning steps that lead to wisdom formation. The world needs wisdom. As advocates of Black youth, it is imperative to engage in intentional efforts to help form them in wisdom.

Part Two and chapter six in particular describes a vision of discipleship education for African American youth. This vision lays the ground work for the Repertory with Roots pedagogy of engagement. The foundation of this vision is wisdom, and provides perspective on teaching and learning with Black youth that is relational, real and relevant.

### Wisdom Defined

There are three definitions of wisdom that call for our consideration, the fear of God, God as the source of wisdom, and the necessity of wisdom when growing as a Christian disciple. Author Robert Fleming shares, wisdom is a commentary on our times. Political and social parallels between the eras of the elders and our own are sources from which to learn.[96] Stated another way, wisdom is an act of discernment. Fleming's definition suggests that over time patterns and habits repeat themselves. Indeed, there is nothing new under the sun.[97] The supposed author of Ecclesiastes, Qohelet is acutely aware of what's going on in the world, and his teachings are marked by continual interaction between traditional theology and the concerns of contemporary life.[98] He writes about wisdom throughout the entire book. The term "under the sun," is the author's way of referring to experience in this life, there is no distinction between past and future.[99]

Knowing and discerning the history of African diasporic people should inform our understanding of current actions and ideas. For example, witnessing the killings of unarmed Black men by white law enforcement officers in the twenty-first century should cause us to reflect on the lives of Black predecessors such as Emmett Till and others who also died at the hands of white racists. Wisdom encourages an embrace of values that demonstrate a fear of God as well as love and respect for others and ourselves. Wisdom is living in ways that acknowledge the struggles of those who have gone before. Today senseless violence permeates Black communities. Black youth are killing each other at greater rates than the Ku Klux Klan did in a period of more than a hundred years. Wisdom calls for a change in the way we are treating one another. As an African American Christian community it is important to honor, trust, respect, love and protect each other and teach children and youth to do the same.

Minister and author Linda Hollies refers to Proverbs 1:20 and names wisdom "Lady Wisdom," Hollies says that Lady Wisdom's words are not just suggestions, her education is not to be ignored, and she is not just a storyteller or teacher of parables. The proverbs she shares are counsel that has been lived and passed down from generation to generation.[100] Lady Wisdom's counsel comes from God. In fact, she was brought forth as the first of the Lord's works. She was formed at the very beginning, when the world came to be.[101] Wisdom as described by Dr. Hollies has existed since the beginning of time. She calls for Christians to be quiet and listen, for God's wisdom can be found all around us. It can be heard in the voices of children, the words of the elders, the still small voice of God, as well as the forces of nature. Although, I am not suggesting every person, place or thing possesses wise character or instruction, we discover, discern and decide what is and what it is not through vast and diverse people, places and things. Hollies highlights that the most important thing we can acquire is wisdom that comes from God. Wisdom teaches that the most important foundation we build in life is moral character that honors God.

A third consideration of wisdom evolved out of a conversation between my mentor Dr. Anne Wimberly and me, which focused on the question, "What is wisdom?"[102] After thinking and bouncing ideas back and forth we concluded that wisdom is essential for the development of youth as Christian disciples. It is the ability to make sound choices and good decisions. Wisdom is intelligence shaped by experience. It is information softened by understanding. Wisdom is scarce and Christian educators must intentionally focus on wisdom formation in our churches. Wisdom formation is a process of discipleship. We must decipher how to live lives committed to God. Our words, actions and thoughts should demonstrate that devotion. Wisdom is deliberate and takes place throughout the course of one's life. Identifying wisdom as a lifelong pursuit demonstrates the need for Black elders and Black youth to work collectively to address the wisdom deficiency that exists in the Black community.

## The African American Wisdom Tradition

Wisdom in the African American tradition is not simply knowledge; rather it is those insights, attitudes, beliefs and behaviors and practices that create and sustain a life of hope and that produce an inherent sense of self-worth in oneself.[103] In my family and countless others, growing in wisdom requires listening to people who live with a sense of purpose and commitment to something bigger than themselves. People of African descent were unwilling immigrants to the new world, who chose to lift themselves out of the pits of slavery, endured the degrading acts of second-class citizenship, and the atrocities of Jim Crow to build a better life not only for themselves but for generations yet unborn. This is an integral display of wisdom upon which the legacy of African American history and culture is built.

Somehow, the African American community seems to have lost its way. In many respects we have dropped the baton that our ancestors ran with so faithfully and with fortitude. The descendants of African kings and queens appear to have lost their crowns, but that's only a mirage when you consider the wisdom and hope of God. A wise poet whose lips exude the nectar of wisdom proclaims this wisdom and hope. Minister, psychologist and poet Dr. Thema Simone Bryant Davis says:

"Your crown has only been misplaced. It is not erased. The ancestors and angels have not forgotten who you are. They've seen your true place among the stars. Just be still and look within. The most high has already begun to mend; those broken places and fill those empty spaces. Stop living below your potential and put back on your crown. It's time for you to soar again for your home is not the ground."[104]

For Black people and black youth in particular, putting on our crowns is going to take the combined wisdom of Mama, Daddy, Granny, Papa, Madea, Unc, Auntie, Baby Girl, Baby Boy, Sister, Brother, Cuz, the good Reverend Doctor and others who personify the "sage" in our families and communities. We are in desperate need of "wise ones" who will interact with, intercede on behalf of and engage today's Black youth. With this being noted, I must acknowledge the inherent problem that oftentimes prevents this wisdom sharing from taking place. Black youth have very distinctive ways of expressing themselves. Because of this, they may appear to be disinterested, disengaged, disruptive and disrespectful when interacting with those sharing wisdom. Nevertheless, Proverbs 22: 6 instructs "Direct children onto the right path, and when they are older they will not leave it."[105] Stated differently, when youth are formed in wisdom, they will one day walk in wisdom. Walking alongside Black youth as they sojourn through the perils and pitfalls, triumphs and joys of adolescence imparting words of wisdom and living faithful lives before them is a form of "keeping it real." This kind of realness requires an embrace of what cultural critic bell hooks calls engaged pedagogy,[106] where teaching and learning connects with the overall life experiences of Black youth.

Considering the role of the Black church in the wisdom formation of Black youth, engaging and connecting on a real level presents a practical pedagogical challenge, regarding the struggle to be relevant. The Black church must do a better job of helping young people to become rooted in the knowledge and experience of who God is and how God acts in their lives. To facilitate this understanding in the lives of Black youth, the church must give particular attention to the process of Christian wisdom formation known as discipleship.

## Christian Wisdom Formation

Christian wisdom formation is a process of discipleship that is appropriate, relevant and clearly needed in this present era. Discipleship is a way of living that follows the life and teachings of Jesus Christ. According to Dr. Anne Streaty Wimberly and Dr. Evelyn L. Parker, Christian wisdom formation is a continual exploration that calls persons to acknowledge that the ministry and teachings of Jesus Christ are "perpetually reborn" in one's life.[107] The wisdom formation of youth is essential to the discipleship process because it equips them with an awareness and understanding of who they are as followers of Jesus Christ. Wisdom formation is a key element of both contextualized education and the development of one's voice. Christian wisdom formation is an avenue for youth to grow in their understanding of what it means to be a disciple of Jesus Christ through intentional reflection and engagement with Black history, Black culture, Black music and the Bible. These elements are essential to Christian wisdom formation.

The work of three pioneering African American Christian Educators has laid a foundation for the Repertory with Roots Pedagogy of Engagement—Dr. Grant Shockley, Dr. Yolanda Smith and Dr. Anne Wimberly. Their work represents examples of tested educational theories through which the distinctiveness of the Black tradition is preserved. Shockley considers the importance of social justice. Smith highlights the necessity of music in African American Christian education. Wimberly raises the importance of story and the presence of elders and youth in community. Together, their labor makes a significant contribution to the foundation of this teaching model that integrates history, culture, music and the Bible.

The foundational understandings of Christian wisdom formation presented by Shockley, Smith and Wimberly provide a wealth of insight shared through theology, music and story. Together they engage in Christian education that ministers to the whole person. Shockley, Smith and Wimberly have enriched my understanding of the nature of African American wisdom formation. Prior to exploring their theoretical convictions and practical applications, I had compartmentalized concepts of African American wisdom and formation. African American denoted a particular group of people with experiences particular to their lived reality in America. Wisdom delineated common sense and good judgment. Formation described the process of being shaped. However, following a thorough exploration of their work, my understanding has broadened. African American wisdom formation is a critical concept that serves as a foundation for the holistic growth and development of Black youth as Disciples of Christ. It serves as a roadmap with cultural distinctives that stress the importance of making sound decisions based on biblical truths and theological constructs which lead to maturation as one experiences the living of life.

Christian educator Grant Shockley supports the view that Christian education in the Black church should embrace liberation and be significant to the cultural heritage of African diasporic people. His view is that there is a fundamental need for Black churches to develop curricular frameworks that focus on African American experience through "intentional engagement."[108] The intentional engagement model embraces theological reflection and includes six steps:

1) *Conceptualization* helps students understand the biblical message in relation to the situations of their lives as well as gain an understanding of how God is present and active in their situation.[109]
2) *Awareness* helps students become consciously aware of the circumstances and forces that prohibit their liberation.[110]
3) *Analysis* helps students develop the skill and ability to analyze various dimensions of oppression and decide whether to pursue freedom or remain in bondage.
4) *Re-evaluation* engages students in introspective reflection that prompts them to consider their situation and pursue self or social liberation.[111]
5) *Praxis* invites students to engage in responsible action stemming from the new ideas encountered during the previous steps.[112]
6) *Community* results from students growing together, sharing and becoming committed to liberation and change.[113]

Shockley's model has the potential to point African American youth toward a transformed relationship with God, whereby they embrace the radical ministry of Jesus Christ and become empowered to bring transformation in their lives and the lives of others. This model points to the central role of youth in their own wisdom formation. It suggests that if wisdom forming discipleship education is to lead to the formation and wise action of youth on their own and other's behalf, then they must be wholly invested in the educational process. The Intentional Engagement model supports an intergenerational community that embraces youth, hearing them and acting with them and on their behalf. In sum, Shockley presents a model that evokes exceedingly helpful insights for a vision of Christian education directed towards Black youth's growing in wisdom and discipleship.

Christian educator Yolanda Smith uses music as a pathway for growing in wisdom. She contributes the "triple heritage model"[114] of Christian education as a foundational understanding of African American Wisdom Formation. Its three basic components allow African Americans to preserve and celebrate their African, African American and Christian heritages. Smith believes that African history and heritage serves as a catalyst for African Americans to embrace their African roots. Black History highlights the important ways in which African Americans have contributed to the advancement of American society. Christian heritage alerts African Americans to Jewish and Christian traditions that inform their faith, yet also encourages them to be proud of the unique characteristics that African American Christianity embraces.[115] Smith uses spirituals, which were the songs of Black slaves in early America to teach within the Triple Heritage model. The model is "communal, creative, critical and cooperative;" it draws the community together by incorporating creative teaching methodology allowing for critical participation that inspires toward action.[116]

The formation of wisdom happens in community. Community engagement also provides Black youth with the opportunity to communicate, learn and dialogue with each other on various topics of the Christian faith. Considering my vision of discipleship education as a wisdom forming endeavor, a curriculum that considers the Triple Heritage model has the potential to develop in youth an authentic sense of community. Youth can connect with each other and connect with the elders—teachers/leaders as the Body of Christ. Discipleship education for Christian wisdom formation assists youth in discovering their uniqueness as disciples of Jesus Christ. Using imaginative methods to discover their one-of-a-kind identity is integral to the vision. Drawing from the creative messages in music, biblical stories and life stories, Black youth are afforded the opportunity to uncover the possibilities of their lives in concert with others. Creative exploration of worldview and theological messages in Black music has the potential to push youth toward being change agents in their communities.

The power of story is central to creative educational approaches as affirmed by Christian educator Anne Wimberly. She has created the story-linking model of Christian education as a foundational understanding of African American wisdom formation. She describes story-linking as a series of actions wherein students of Christian education link their life stories with biblical stories and stories of prominent African Americans in history.[117] By bridging their stories, Black youth connect themselves to role models who lived in community and were influenced by the message of the Gospel. This linkage occurs by way of the four phases of the story-linking model:[118]

1) *Engaging the everyday story* involves Black youth bringing their own stories to the community as they explore the Christian life.
2) *Engaging the Christian faith story in the Bible* links with biblical stories in the Old or New Testament to the everyday stories of Black youth.
3) *Engaging Christian faith stories from the African American Heritage* connects components of the everyday life story with stories from the African American Christian faith heritage.
4) *Engaging participants in Christian ethical decision making* encourages Black youth to pull together insights and reflections from the first three phases.[119]

In considering the usefulness of the story-linking model for youth wisdom formation, it is important to note that stories can be told through a variety of mediums. This means we can and should use narratives, music, sermons, poems, prayers, artwork and other mediums that tell stories about African American history, culture, music and faith.

The next chapter continues with the vision of discipleship education by exploring the goals which are designed to give voice to the ideas in the vision. It provides a more nuanced view of the purposes of why this vision of discipleship is integral to African American youth's Christian wisdom formation.[120]

## Chapter Seven

# Being Grounded—Beliefs, Ethics, Theology, Character, History & Culture

*Establishing goals sets a trajectory for moving towards an expected end.*

The goals of discipleship education as Christian wisdom formation have the power to transform the lives of today's Black youth. Belief formation, ethical embodiment, theological grounding, character development and historical-cultural enlightenment are worthy goals and serve as the identified ends toward which the vision is directed. Goals provide structure and lead to outcomes of discipleship education that meet Black youth in their cultural context and popular culture. Christian Educator Lora Ellen McKinney asserts that discipleship education, done effectively, possesses the ability to inform us about Jesus Christ by highlighting a significant linkage with African American heritage to disprove myths about the faith of African Americans and teach values that are applicable to the lives of African Diasporic people.[121] Discipleship education in the Repertory with Roots model of teaching is organized around five goals:

1) Belief Formation
2) Ethical Embodiment
3) Theological Grounding
4) Character Development
5) Historical-Cultural Enlightenment.

These are worthy goals that meet the need for youth to be transformed in their relationship with God, self and others.

## Belief Formation

Belief formation is having a head and heart knowledge of God, Jesus and the Holy Spirit; this knowledge frames our Christian belief system. A personal experience of God the Father, Jesus the Son and the Holy Spirit holds potential for moving youth beyond knowing about the Trinity to actually knowing and being in relationship with the Trinity. One area in which this occurs is in worship through participation in rituals, symbols and language. Youth are invited to look for moments in worship that engage them in a love and knowledge of God. Youth may connect with a song that speaks to them about the nature of who God is or their lived experience of God; this connection allows them to understand God as more than a theological construct but as a "real" part of their lives as young Christians.

Another area where youth are encouraged to explore a knowledge of God, Jesus and the Holy Spirit is in Bible study. Bible study is a prime opportunity for youth and their teachers/facilitators to absorb lots of head knowledge of the scriptures. However, the more difficult task is to engage them in study sessions where they can move from head knowledge to heart knowledge, which cannot be done without the presence and power of the Holy Spirit. It is the life application of the scriptures that lend itself to transformation. Living the life that the Bible speaks of moves persons toward more Christ-like character. Thematic study, character study, and book-by-book study provides opportunities to live the life that we read about in the word of God.

Belief formation can be understood through the concept of "evocative nurture," proposed by Dr. Anne Wimberly. Evocative nurture is a method that invites us to enter into an experience of knowing the Trinity that moves from intellectual awareness (head knowing) to authentic relationship (heart knowing).[122] Wimberly uses a four part framework in which participants work together to explore and name images and beliefs of God through thinking about God's nature and activity when we listen to or tell stories. By drawing analogies between our lives and the lives of Bible characters we are demonstrating how God was present and acted then as well as now. We can also decipher how God responds to us and how we respond to God. Finally, this framework calls us to examine the ways that we try to control God and it challenges us to release the limitations we put on God.[123] This framework demonstrates how a person can grow in his or her personal relationship with God, Jesus and the Holy Spirit. It lays a foundation for a life-long journey of being formed in our beliefs.

## Ethical Embodiment

Ethical embodiment involves moral decision making which leads to a lifestyle based on what a person believes and why he or she should act on it. People are commanded to live by the Golden Rule: "Do to others whatever you would like them to do to you."[124] Living according to the Golden Rule requires humanity and devotion to the Christian faith. Those who facilitate a Repertory with Roots educational experience have the primary task of helping Black youth get in touch with the full range of positive and negative images of life and making choices that reflects the Christian lifestyle. Insofar as Christian educators do this, we fulfill the goal of ethical embodiment that liberates youth to embrace and experience spiritual transformation. When persons are in Christ, they are called to walk by the Spirit and life takes on new quality. This means that "anyone who belongs to Christ has become a new person. The old life is gone, a new life has begun."[125] Emphasizing the importance of "walking by the spirit" in one's character and relationships reminds youth that living as Christ's disciple is a continually growing process. Central to the goal is helping youth see that with Christ, they are called to take on a new servant nature, and that walking by the spirit empowers them to live by a different standard of self-giving love. The outcome is their knowing that God's Spirit frees them to serve others.

## Theological Grounding

The goal of theological grounding is the youth's development of a framework that helps them to understand the relationship between God, themselves, humanity and all of creation. This goal is carried out through encounters with the stories of the Bible, the community of faith and the youth's life experiences. The expected outcome is that youth will understand the connection between God, God's creation and themselves: this connection will hopefully lead to a personal relationship with God through Jesus Christ, empowered by the Holy Spirit.

We can examine this outcome through the lens of Black Theology. Methodologically, Black Theologians look at the Black Religious experience to discover the meaning of God's activities in the world. Black Theology is essential to theological grounding for Black youth because it grows out of and centers on encounters, alliances and circumstances that challenge Black people in their daily struggle to survive. It begins with the experiences of African Americans as a starting point in understanding their relationship with God through Jesus Christ. Black Theology suggests that the method necessarily includes constructing a worldview surrounding the experience of Black people as Africans in America. In considering Black Theology as a goal of discipleship education as Christian wisdom formation, we must recognize and acknowledge the key role of scripture in undergirding the Christian life and witness as an integral characteristic of Christian discipleship.

In order to grow in Christian discipleship, youth must not only read the words of scripture but allow the message to touch their spirit and infuse their very being. As disciples, youth are called to approach the scriptures prayerfully and to seek to discern the mind of Christ for their lives and relationships. It is a matter of coming before the word of God asking, "What is God saying to me through this passage of scripture, and what would God have me do in faith in response to this message?" Theological grounding in this light is "doing theology." Theological grounding involves helping youth engage in conversations and story sharing that results in reflecting theologically about God, Jesus and the Holy Spirit and all of God's created world, and how this informs their lives.

In addition to prioritizing scripture, theological grounding assists youth in developing an awareness of communal responsibility, the practice of looking beyond a person's own needs to that of the greater community. It moves youth into the realm of collective responsibility through work that helps and supports others in need. It helps youth transform their theological reflection into practice. Youth are encouraged to understand their life experiences in light of what others go through who may face similar or not so similar circumstances.

## Character Development

Character development calls people to define their fundamental values, and to prioritize and live out their moral principles. The goal of character development is for Black youth to discern how their value system connects with living a Christ-centered life in light of the influences, pressures and temptations that they face every day. Christian educator Harold Westing offers a helpful method of addressing the crucial issue of character development: his work is based on looking at the recorded ministry of Jesus and his ability to teach Christian character by guiding the disciples and others through experience and example.[126]

He claims that character development exercises help people to be intentional about their character. Westing begins with the assertion that "character must be modeled." Both children and adults are influenced in what they do by observing what those around them do. He also claims that "storytelling influences character." Storytelling is an effective way of teaching a moral lesson. In a manner not unlike Anne Wimberly's story-linking model, Westing supports the view that using scripture to teach a moral lesson gives significance to values being taught. His third point is that "participation by the learner plays a significant role in character development." It is imperative that the teacher/facilitator constructs ways for learners to take active roles in the learning process. Westing also insists that "social interaction needs to occur in a just, moral community." He believes that God can work in any situation in a person's life regardless of the environment, but a just, moral community greatly aids in the learning process. Finally he notes that encouragement reinforces character.[127] Encouragement is important for the youth's self-esteem. It makes them feel good about themselves. In short, the outcome for Black youth is to take on the character of Christ. Methods for achieving this outcome include engaging them in poignant discussions and conversations about the character and values portrayed in popular culture and how these characteristics interface with their lives as Christian disciples. Westing's framework is important to ministry with Black youth because there is a gap between what youth may know as right actions and the life they live. There is also a gap between what is taught in youth ministry settings and the lifestyles of youth. Repertory teachers/facilitators must work for change in this area.

## Historical-Cultural Enlightenment

Teaching and motivating youth to retell the stories of the culture and history of African Diasporic people leads to a historically and culturally enlightened constituency of Black youth. Engaging in teaching and learning experiences like this is the goal of helping Black youth to understand the Black historical and cultural experience. To facilitate this awareness, the pilgrimage and heritage of Afro-centric persons must be told so that youth comprehend the multi-faceted cultural and historical life of Black people. The expected outcome of recounting the legacy of African Americans is the youth's development of an appreciation of Black history and culture and its narrative struggle of a people. Fostering historical cultural enlightenment requires a method of teaching Black history, Black culture, Black church history and contemporary issues from the Black perspective.

Christian educator Dr. Oliva Pearl Stokes a staunch supporter of historical-cultural enlightenment for African American people, particularly children and youth supports the view that theological truths from the field of Black Theology should be communicated in Christian education contexts. Following this view, Stokes claims the relevance of affirming one's blackness as a source for positive development among Black Christians.[128] She draws upon the rich heritage of African and African American traditions and explores and develops new models of religious education that demonstrated a "problem centered" or "this worldly" method for use in religious education. Dr. Stokes maintains that education in the Black church must take an active role in addressing the "real" problems encountered by African Americans and the church's educational ministry must concern itself with holistic ways of living.[129] Dr. Stokes ideas contribute greatly to my belief that knowing who you are culturally and historically enriches one's experience as a Christian. Moreover, her perceptions parallel the identity of the unashamedly Black and unapologetic Christian.

Learning about and engaging in activities that foster historical-cultural enlightenment become a necessary goal of contemporary youth ministry because it helps to construct a positive racial identity. Often Black youth's knowledge of Black history and culture begins and ends with slavery. Their knowledge lacks a well-rounded examination of African American history and culture amidst the horrors of slavery, lynching, Jim Crow and segregation. Black history and culture is a story of triumph in the midst of tragedy and pain. Black history and culture have built this country (United States), and we must communicate it to Black youth, and commission them to retell the stories to their peers and others Youth in today's world is that they transcend the negative associations that are a part of their context. They need to be taught about the historical and cultural legacy of people of African descent because this legacy reveals the strength that emerges from the struggle.

The five goals—belief formation, ethical embodiment, theological grounding, character development and historical-cultural enlightenment form a vision of discipleship education as Christian wisdom formation for Black youth. The goals provide direction for the creation of the Repertory with Roots pedagogy of engagement and point to expected outcomes. The goals do not stand alone. There is a need for the kinds of methods that give rise to goal implementation. One element that is pivotal is the development of outcomes that engage youth in creative exploration as well as critical thinking and awareness. Important to this methodology is moving from oppression to liberation. This move is important because it moves youth from being mindless consumers of popular culture to serious advocates of hope and liberation in today's and tomorrow's world. In sum, creative exploration, critical thinking and awareness serve as a bridge that carries youth from the realm of inexperience to the realm of experience as they engage, decipher and discuss Black history, Black culture, Black music and the Bible.

# Chapter Eight

# Living It Out—Study, Prayer, Worship, Service, Mentoring

*Christian practices help us deepen our awareness of God's presence in our lives; starting us on a journey of practicing the presence of God with others.*

Christian practices should be shared in community. They point beyond the individualism that is so dominant in today's society. Through sharing in practices, the quality of our lives as Christians is enhanced. Our theology is sharpened, our spirituality is heightened and our thinking evolves. We unite with God and one another in a communion of fellowship where grace, mercy and God's presence abounds.

## Practices of Discipleship Education as Christian Wisdom Formation

A set of practices is necessary to facilitate the implementation of the goals and associated methods presented in chapter 7. In this chapter, a set of practices will be introduced for use in youth ministry settings that focus on discipleship education as a Christian wisdom formation endeavor. Christian practices are activities that Christian people do together in order to grow in their relationship with God and each other. Practical Theologians Dorothy Bass and Don Richter share several key concepts in understanding how to effectively engage in Christian practices. They contend that Christian practices include persons in God's work in the world as an impression of the love and grace of God.[130] These practices should be done with and learned from others. They are not done only within the church but in homes, schools and communities. They are integral to Christian faith.[131] Appropriate spiritual and educational practices are essential for Black youths' discipleship and Christian wisdom formation. In order for Christian discipleship formation to happen, Black youth must enter into life-informing, life-affirming, and life-changing practices. Life-informing practices teach about life. Life-affirming practices support what youth already know about life. Life-changing practices alter the manner in which youth carry out their life's mission. Practices to be presented here that are deemed to be life-informing, life-affirming and life-changing include study, prayer, worship, service and mentoring.

## Study

Of all the practices that are described in the following sections, study is central to the Repertory with Roots pedagogy of engagement on which this book is centered. A pedagogy of engagement refers to education that focuses on connecting teaching and learning with the overall experiences of African American youth. This does not negate the other practices, but the prominence of study stems from my observation that the study of scripture does not necessarily connect to the life experiences of today's Black youth. At the very center of critical reflection is the necessity of study.

Study is the deliberate practice of engaging the mind with the scriptures and the world God has created in such a way that the mind is changed completely.[132] Study is integral to belief formation and theological grounding. Through Bible study we gain insights into the nature of God and God's relationship to all of creation. Studying the scriptures empowers persons to live in a manner that reflects a growing relationship with God and others.[133] Dorothy Bass calls study "getting lost in the story," and when we enter God's story, we remember who and whose we are.[134] Like Dr. Anne Wimberly, Bass affirms the necessity of story on our journey as Christians. Both substantiate a call for Christian education that centers on story. Bass believes that all persons have a place in God's story and are called to share the transforming power of that story with others.[135] Wimberly declares the importance of bringing our own stories to the teaching and learning setting and prompts persons to consider how their stories connect with God's story in ways that lead to liberation and hope as they journey through life, emphasizing that persons must share their stories, examine them critically and ascertain mature choices.[136]

Connecting youths' stories with the biblical story helps them to witness God's presence and action in their lives. Getting into the story causes the story to get into the youth and form the way that they live. Bass invites youth to not only read and study the story but also to think of themselves as part of the story. Wimberly admonishes youth not to isolate their stories from God's story, but rather to identify ways in which God is present and active among them. Both theorists present the relevance and necessity of story in today's Christian education contexts. Through careful and critical interaction with Black history, culture, music and the Bible youth are exposed to the roots of the pedagogy which promote growth and change through the practice of study.

## Prayer

Prayer is the practice of communicating with God. It is talking to and hearing from God. The practice of prayer provides opportunities for persons to spend time with God throughout the day.[137] The early church recognized that prayer was essential to the spiritual life of the individual and the development of a strong body of believers. This practice contributed to belief formation in the past and continues to do so today. Through engaging in regular prayer times, youth gain a sense of the importance of this spiritual practice. Prayer helps youth become increasingly aware of the transcendent presence that is bigger than themselves.

Understanding that prayer was a tool to help them become stronger followers of Christ, the disciples asked, "Lord teach us to pray."[138] Likewise, this is a statement that our youth should be encouraged to pursue because it cannot be assumed that youth know how to pray. There are models and tools for prayer that I encourage as methods for youth to engage in the practice of prayer. The A.C.T.S. and J.O.Y. models provide a basic typology for prayer foci. A.C.T.S. is an acronym for prayers of adoration, confession, thanksgiving and supplication. J.O.Y. encourages prayers to Jesus, for others and yourself.

Anne Wimberly discusses the importance of prayer as a spiritual practice that "nurtures faith and hope."[139] She says persons develop a soul language whereby they talk to God. Prayer is an opportunity for young people to build their own prayer language and enter into conversations with God through which they learn about who God is, how God acts in their lives, their own need for relationship with God, and their ways of responding to God. Identifying prayer as an act of self-disclosure before God makes prayer a nurturing experience.

Prayer is a common experience among people of faith. There is a sense that to pray is as natural as to eat, drink, breathe and sleep. Persons cry out to God in the face of difficulty or pain or utter spontaneous expressions of thanksgiving when they encounter unexpected blessings. The tendency to pray is built into them; however, an inclination to pray is different from an ongoing practice of prayer. Living a life of prayer or praying consistently is not easy. Living a life of prayer requires commitment and discipline. This must be taught and practiced in order for youth to grow in the life of discipleship. Providing consistent opportunities for youth to practice and engage in prayer is of great benefit. Prayer allows for youth to express their displeasure and disgust as well as hopes and dreams for Black people to a God who hears and answers prayer. Prayer helps youth to mature in wisdom as they seek the heart of God.

## Worship

Worship is a practice that begins with acknowledging who God is and what God has done in the life of God's people.[140] In the assembled community, worshipers offer praise, thanksgiving, honor and glory to God. Worship contributes to belief formation, theological grounding, and character development through, song, prayer, scripture and sermon. Affirming and engaging in the practice of worship as part of Christian discipleship formation brings about renewal in youths' lives of faith. There is something transforming about the experience of worshipping God. Worshipers focus on the goodness, grace, presence and strength of God in their lives: in worship people are lifted beyond themselves and their circumstances into the presence of God.

According to Wimberly, Christian worship is largely considered to be an essential educational ministry practice that nourishes one's faith.[141] Worship creates an atmosphere of faith and hope for youth. Because of the artistry contained in African American culture, youth may desire to create and implement their own style of worship services. Through participation in planning and leading worship, God invites youth to be a part of something far greater than themselves—the kingdom of God.

## Service

Being formed in wisdom requires that one have a servant's heart. Christian minister Adele Calhoun asserts that service is a way of sharing one's possessions, time, money, influence and skill in caring for, protecting and developing others.[142] A disciple demonstrates servanthood by helping others in practical ways. Through serving others, one represents the true essence of discipleship. The Bible emphasizes serving others, and Jesus taught his followers to be servants.[143] The practice of servanthood includes being willing to do routine tasks, being available to God and to those one is called to serve. This practice also includes being observant and alert to the needs of others and occasionally doing more than is asked. True servants do what they are supposed to do and more.

When we help youth engage in service, the purpose is to assist them in understanding that they are not merely pew warmers; rather God has called them to put their faith into action. Underscoring the importance of living out discipleship in deeds of compassion and justice helps to create a connection between belief and practice. The Christian faith is a working faith. It is a faith that manifests itself in loyalty to Jesus Christ, a faith that obeys Christ's teachings, and a faith that serves one's neighbor.[144] In an important way, this practice mirrors Dr. Grant Shockley's emphasis on service as social justice ministry. Through ongoing involvement in social justice learning, an awareness of the social mission of the biblical message is identified. Also central to understanding the practice of service is the view that one's faith in Jesus should inform and motivate one's actions. African American youth are challenged to live out their discipleship through service.

To support the importance of the practice of service, Dr. Yolanda Smith uses the term "returning service."[145] "Returning service" means being an active participant in the life of the community that has helped that person to become who they are. It also requires that one gives back to the community that exerted influence in their life.[146] This is achieved through what Smith calls "directed action." She describes it as deliberate action aimed at progressing towards "social, economic, political, spiritual and physical" transformation in the community.[147] This understanding of the practice of service also corresponds with Dr. Evelyn Parker's theory of emancipatory hope. It prepares African American youth to serve as leaders, which empowers them to critically examine and voice their concerns about the oppressive structures of race, class and sex.[148] As developing leaders, Black youth are called to serve humanity and to live out this calling as Christians.[149]

## Mentoring

Mentoring is a one-to-one relational commitment that persists over a long period of time between two people. Often, the mentor is an older, wiser adult and the mentee is a young person. This relationship helps to provide constant encouragement, guidance and help as the youth experiences difficult situations in life.[150] Mentoring assists the younger person in gaining the skills and confidence necessary to be responsible for his or her own future. According to Wimberly and Christian educator Dr. Maisha Handy, mentoring is best practiced with a "wisdom guide" who through affirmation and action passes on Christian principles, knowledge and a "blueprint for Christian living" to the one seeking wisdom.[151] They describe the mentor as a trusted friend and guide, who shares insights, provides assessment of various situations preserves the honor of the relationship, models appropriate conduct and is committed to the spiritual growth and health of the mentee.[152]

The practice of mentoring underscores the reality that wisdom formation of Black youth cannot be separated from the Black family context. This context, known as the "village" describes unity that exists within the community, and encourages the development of a "valued identity" that engenders hope in the midst of life's difficulties.[153] It is from the "village" that wisdom guides emerge. Within the village, individual mentoring relationships and the values they promote find communal reinforcement. Because of the breakdown of the family structure and lack of community engagement, youth need to reestablish the "village" context. Youth need wise adults who will impart knowledge and wisdom in their lives. The practice of mentoring can contribute to belief formation, theological grounding, ethical embodiment, character development and historical-cultural enlightenment as mentors facilitate learning and practical engagement in each area. Mentors in the faith can serve as guides who engage in critical discussion with youth about Black history, culture, music and the Bible and who prompt them to make wise decisions regarding their involvement with contemporary culture.

The practices of study, prayer, worship, service and mentoring create a comprehensive framework of practices needed to carry out the goals and methods of discipleship education for African American youth. When youth engage them faithfully and consistently, these practices have the potential to help youth grow in Christian wisdom formation. Repertory with Roots can easily incorporate the aforementioned practices in the curriculum's content and methodology. This merger of practices brings unity, fellowship and transformation as the "village" comes together in study.

## Unit Summary

Chapters 6, 7 and 8 described a vision of discipleship as a Christian wisdom formation endeavor for African American youth. These chapters examine the foundational understandings of African American wisdom formation and Christian discipleship in the work of Christian educators Grant Shockley, Yolanda Smith and Anne Wimberly. They identify goals and associated methods for carrying out the vision of discipleship education as Christian wisdom formation and they describe key practices needed to facilitate the implementation of those goals and associated methods.

The vision outlined in this unit, with added attention to goals, associated methods and practices provides a blueprint for "real ministry" with Black youth. What I have included in this chapter expresses my passion for what needs to happen with Black youth living in contemporary culture. It also demonstrates my commitment to assist these youth in their spiritual, emotional, social, intellectual, emotional, physical and moral development. Of primary importance to this vision is the development of the whole person. When woven together, the discipleship goals of belief formation, ethical embodiment, theological grounding, character development and historical-cultural enlightenment create a paradigm for African-centered Christian education that engages the holistic nature of African American youth. Black history, culture, music and the Bible play an important role in this vision. The pivotal role of Black music stems from the powerful manner in which it defines African American culture, and informs the knowledge, attitudes and behaviors of youth growing up in that culture. This unit provides a framework for envisioning a model of youth ministry designed for Black youth that is relational, real and relevant.

## Part 3

# The Repertoire—Constructing a Pedagogy

## Chapter Nine

# The Roots of a Pedagogy—Building from the Ground Up

*"I am where I am because of the bridges that I crossed. Sojourner Truth was a bridge. Ida B. Wells was a bridge. Madame C.J. Walker was a bridge. Fannie Lou Hamer was a bridge."*[154]

These words of truth spoken by Oprah Winfrey tell the story of all of our lives. We are where we are because someone has been the connector from one place to another. Teaching and learning embody the same criteria. Those who learn teach. Those who teach learn. Both join us to the world of the greater. Greater knowledge, greater blessings, greater joy, greater peace, greater wisdom, greater service, and the list could continue. Teaching and learning are my calling and my passions. I am thankful to serve as a bridge connecting Black youth with their history, culture, music and the word of God through Christian education I pray that these youth will grow in their relationship with Jesus Christ. This chapter describes in detail, The Repertory with Roots pedagogy of engagement, the bridge that provides Black youth the opportunity to explore Black history, Black culture, Black music and the Bible through a creative framework whose intention is to help them grow in their identity and transform their lives.

Pedagogy is a curricular design that refers to how a teacher orchestrates teaching and learning. Repertory with Roots is a model of teaching that focuses on discipleship education for Christian wisdom formation. Repertory with Roots incorporates the elements of Black history, Black culture, Black music and the Bible. It enhances youth's understanding of who and whose they are. It is an instructional method that fosters belief formation, ethical embodiment, theological grounding, character development and historical-cultural enlightenment. This teaching and learning model affords youth the opportunity to participate in activities that embrace their learning styles and helps them create meaning through relating new information to what they already know.

The pedagogy consists of seven methodological movements—inviting, listening, connecting, engaging, exploring, emerging, and honoring. I use the term movements because this pedagogy comprises an interactive learning experience that embraces motion and reciprocal exchange between the youth and the session facilitators. Here dialogue flows freely; discussions are arranged so that all persons must participate in the process.[155]

Before engaging and exploring the pedagogical framework, however we will consider learning styles, multiple intelligences and tips for leading discussions. These components assist in developing transformative teaching and learning experiences with the Repertory with Roots curricular design. Theories on learning styles and multiple intelligences remind us of the diverse ways that learning takes place in all of us. Preparing great questions creates a foundation for rich and meaningful discussions on Black history, Black culture, Black music and the Bible with Black youth.

## Learning Styles

We all learn in different ways. Each person God creates makes sense of information in his or her own unique and preferred fashion. Seeing and perceiving information in a manner that is understandable to that person is called a learning style. Building the Repertory with Roots pedagogy of engagement begins with the premise that the teaching and learning methodology must be presented in a manner in which students can understand and engage the content in a way that fits who they are and how they learn best.

Christian educator Marlene LeFever provides insight on how people learn in her book, *"Learning Styles: Reaching Everyone God Gave You to Teach."* She identifies four learning styles—imaginative, analytic, common sense and dynamic. Imaginative learners learn best in contexts that allow for interpersonal communication. They are curious, love to ask questions and learn best by listening and sharing ideas. Imaginative learners are big picture thinkers rather than detail oriented. They will ask the question: Why study this?

The analytic learner learns by watching and listening. They expect a teacher to stand before them and to present information while they carefully assess the value of the information presented. Analytic learners learn in the way most teachers have traditionally taught, through lecture or teacher-directed presentations. They are quiet in class. They are listeners. They like to work in a quiet atmosphere. Analytic learners aim for perfection. Before making a decision, they want to know all of the information necessary. They ask the question: What do I need to know?

Common sense learners like to play with ideas to see if they are rational and workable. They want to test theory in the real world, and apply what they have learned. Common sense learners are hands-on people who use their own ideas to analyze and solve problems. They excel when engaging in practical tasks, and they learn best when learning is combined with doing. Common sense learners ask the question: How does this work?

Dynamic learners also enjoy activity as part of the learning process. However, they excel in following their hunches, sensing new directions and examining new possibilities. They are risk takers that thrive on situations that call for flexibility and change. Dynamic learners love to start new things and put their personal stamp of originality on an idea. They ask the question: What can this become?[156]

Within each learning style, students learn through various types of activities—auditory (hearing), visual (seeing), or tactile/kinesthetic (feeling/doing). For example, you may have an imaginative learner who responds more eagerly to pictures or videos. Common sense learners may fit into more tactile or hands-on activity. An analytic learner may respond to a sermon. Each student has a different combination of style and activity by which he or she learns best. Before engaging the experiential lessons shared in the appendices, start with your own exploration of learning style preferences. Read each description again. Are you an imaginative, analytic, common sense or dynamic learner? Do you prefer more auditory, visual or tactile/kinesthetic activities? Which descriptions fit you best? There is no wrong answer. Just keep in mind that most teachers teach the way they learn best. It is crucial that you move beyond that comfort zone and try new possibilities in order to reach your students. Recognizing your own learning style will help you reach out to all your students through intentional effort when designing teaching and learning experiences.

**Multiple Intelligences: Eight Ways of Learning**

Educational Researcher, Howard Gardner used his book *"Multiple Intelligences: Theory and Practice"* to introduce the term "intelligence" rather than learning styles. He asks teachers to rethink processes that facilitate learning, especially among students who learn in different ways. Gardner's theory of multiple intelligences suggests there are eight intelligences. They are linguistic, logical mathematical, spatial, bodily-kinesthetic, musical, interpersonal, intrapersonal and naturalist.[157]

Teaching becomes stronger and more effective when the leader considers multiple intelligences. At least one question should emerge from each intelligence that assists in lesson planning. Those with linguistic intelligence are word smart. They have highly developed auditory skills. These learners enjoy reading and writing. While preparing, one should consider how to use the written and spoken word in my lesson. Those gifted with the logical-mathematical intelligence are number smart. They like to explore patterns and solve problems. Teachers considering the logical-mathematical intelligence should ask how they can bring in numbers, calculations, logic, classifications, or critical thinking skills into the lesson. Persons who have spatial intelligence are picture smart. They enjoy art activities and think with images and pictures. When planning to teach those considering spatial intelligence should ask how to use visual aids, visualization, color, art or metaphor. Being gifted with bodily-kinesthetic intelligence is to be body smart. These learners use their bodies in unique and skilled ways. They like to act things out and prefer hands-on learning. If teachers prepare with these learners in mind, they may ask how to use the whole body or include a hands-on experience. Persons with musical intelligence are music smart. They enjoy music and understand the structure of music. If teachers are considering musical intelligences they should think about how they can bring music or environmental sounds or set points in a rhythmic or melodic framework. Those gifted with interpersonal intelligence are people smart. They enjoy group activities and are good at collaborating and incorporating. If one prepares with them in mind, one might plan to engage students in peer sharing, cooperative learning or large group activity. Those with intrapersonal intelligence are self-smart. They are tuned into their own world and like to work independently. While preparing for these learners a teacher should ask how he or she could evoke personal feelings or memories or give student's choices. Finally, persons with the naturalist intelligence are nature smart. They are tuned into the world of nature; they like to be outside and like taking care of pets or plants. For these students, teachers might ask how they can incorporate living things, natural phenomena, or ecological awareness into the lesson.

Although learners will be highly developed in some, modestly developed in others and underdeveloped in the rest, all students will exhibit all eight ways of learning, and many will be developed to a level of competency. Additionally, practicing these different intelligences, even if they are not naturally strengths, will benefit all learners by encouraging learners to explore different learning styles and understand concepts in different ways.[158]

## Discussion: How to Ask Great Questions

Students want to talk. Most students come to youth group for relationships and conversation. Leading a great discussion during a lesson is an awesome way to engage youth. It also serves as a method of accomplishing teaching and learning goals. Discussions can enhance communication skills, invite learning from a variety of sources, and actively engage learner's brains cells.[159] As exciting as discussions can be, there are also a few drawbacks. First, discussions can take up too much time. Second, discussions sometimes ramble off subject. Third, individuals can dominate discussion. Fourth, introverts and other process thinkers may be left out.[160] Nonetheless, the opportunity for learning during discussions, particularly well-prepared ones, outweighs the drawbacks.

Leading a great discussion takes work. Preparing and asking great questions is important. What your students get out of discussion has everything to do with the quality of questions you ask. Christian educator Dan Lambert shares several kinds of questions in his book, "*Teaching That Makes a Difference: How to Teach for Holistic Impact.*" He identifies six types of questions—factual, open, interpretive, thought, evaluation and application.[161] One might use these types of questions as a model to approach writing questions. In the following list, the types of questions, the definition of the types, and example of each type (focused on the parable of the Lost Son as found in Luke 15: 11-32) is provided.

1. **Factual questions** ask for a definite answer that has only one response. Example: Who are the characters in this story?
2. **Open questions** are those that have more than one potential answer. Open questions can fit into any one of the remaining groups.
3. **Interpretive questions** require students to make sense of information. Example: What did the lost son hope to gain by leaving his father's house?
4. **Thought questions** require students to think beyond the specific information in the lesson. Example: What other characters in scripture can you think of that walked away from the Father's (God) protection?
5. **Evaluation questions** push students to figure out why something happened. Example: How are the younger son's actions like our actions today?
6. **Application questions** allow students to think about how the subject matter might make a difference to them. Example: What can you learn from the father about forgiveness?

Another framework that develops higher order thinking skills is Bloom's Taxonomy and Discussion Questions.[162] Educational Psychologist, Dr. Benjamin Bloom developed a way of understanding six levels of thinking that build on each other. It may help to think of Bloom's taxonomy as a staircase.[163] The lower the level (bottom of staircase), the less complex the thinking. Thinking ability moves through more complex and abstract levels to the highest order (top of staircase). Using Bloom's ideas, as lessons develop, teachers should ask questions that move students up the staircase. Listed below are types of questions listed lowest level to highest, and their definitions as well as a sample question based on the story of Mary and Martha found in Luke 10: 38-42:

- **Knowledge questions** allow students to recount previously learned materials by recalling facts, terms, basic concepts and answers.[164] Example: Who are the key people involved in this passage?
- **Comprehension questions** allow students to demonstrate understanding of facts and ideas by organizing, comparing, translating, interpreting, giving descriptions and main points.[165] Example: What did Martha say to Jesus?
- **Application questions** encourage students to solve problems by applying acquired knowledge, facts, techniques and rules.[166] Example: What did Martha learn about the differences between herself and her sister Mary? Identify one thing that you can do to become more like Mary.
- **Analysis questions** encourage students to examine and break down information into parts by identifying motives or causes, as well as making inferences and finding evidence to support generalizations.[167] Example: Why would Martha complain about Mary knowing her personality and character? What is it about the way God made us that causes some of us to be more like Martha even when we know Mary has been commended for her actions in relationship to Jesus?

- **Synthesis questions** ask students to compile information in a different way by combining elements in new patterns or proposing alternative solutions.[168] Example: What might have happened if Martha had decided to discontinue the preparations and join the group? Imagine a conversation between Martha and Jesus after she confronted Jesus.
- **Evaluation questions** encourage students to present and defend opinions using a set of criteria to make judgments about information, the validity of ideas, or the quality of work.[169] Example: How would you defend Martha's argument to have Mary join her with the preparations?

Both Lambert and Bloom's framework are viable options for preparing discussion questions. As one prepares for and leads discussions, keep the following thoughts in mind:

- Ask questions that are more open than closed.
- Ask one question at a time.
- Prepare questions ahead of time.
- After asking a question, be silent. Allow students time to think.
- Follow up student responses with probing or clarifying questions. What else is on the student's mind?
- Accept student responses as if they were gifts.

Asking great questions leads to great teaching and learning experiences. Writing great questions is a skill to be developed. It gets better with practice. Preparing ahead of time is important, however be willing to show flexibility and move away from your teaching plan if prompted by the Holy Spirit to follow up on student comments and questions.

## Repertory with Roots—The Seven Movements

Making the learning styles come to life takes place through the seven movements which comprises an interactive learning experience that embraces motion and reciprocal exchange among the session participants where dialogue flows freely. Within these movements discussions are arranged so that questions and answers are continually reformulated, and all persons must participate in the process.[170] The movements are inviting, listening, connecting, engaging, exploring, emerging, and honoring.

**Inviting** offers youth the opportunity to join the teaching and learning community. The invitation consists of an opening ritual that encourages teachers and learners to call upon God, Jesus and the Holy Spirit as their ultimate teachers. It is a summons to gather as a community, and it provides an opportunity for participants to celebrate their African, African American and Christian heritages.

For purposes of invitation or gathering youth into community, African and African American quotations, meditations, prayers and litanies are important components and help to focus attention on the goal of the session. The resources signal commitment to Christian education from the African American experience. Importantly, the invitation draws upon the rich heritage of African and African American tradition as a means of helping youth to construct a positive ethnic-cultural and Christian identity.

As a movement, inviting begins with setting a simple altar and lighting a candle. Prayer then serves as a catalyst for inviting God's presence into the midst of the gathered community. Reciprocal components of the opening ritual encourage participants and facilitators to work together communally to invoke God's presence through call and response. A ritual of invitation inspires a sense of community in the educational process. The Repertory with Roots pedagogy of engagement provides space for this type of exchange. As learners experience the invitation, they can sound a "call" for a "response" by others. The invitation summons the community to learn and dialogue in a cooperative fashion.

**Listening** calls for critically hearing a piece of Black music, spoken word, poetry, etc. and paying attention to the lyrics in order to decipher the message and raise the listener's consciousness. Listening to the "everyday story" of the artist is the lens through which we set the agenda for the practice of study. Listening to the stories of African American creative artists enlivens the Repertory with Roots teaching and learning model. Listening is an inescapable necessity in the movements of the pedagogy.

This pivotal nature of listening helps youth discern the positive and negative aspects of Black music in ways that lessen youth's vulnerability to adverse effects. By listening critically to a piece of African American music, youth discover the connections between their lives and the artist's message. Listening critically prompts the community to engage the lyrics and put them into conversation with Black history, culture and the Bible. Listening critically moves the learning community to explore writings from African American heritage or the African American wisdom tradition and to view them in light of the messages in the music. Listening critically fosters the emergence of creative artistic expressions conceived and constructed by the youth. Finally, listening critically calls for an opportunity to honor the time shared and the insights learned.

Critical listening is essential for Christian wisdom formation. Youth's wisdom formation cannot develop without wise listening that gives thoughtful critique of the messages communicated in Black music. Listening to music can call forth powerful emotions that are positive or negative. These emotions differ according to the person's ages and stages. As a result, when various forms of Black music are brought into the church for youth to hear and critique, the members of the faith community may not have a welcoming appreciation for the listening movement. This clash in hearing may have the effect of what Dr. Anne Wimberly calls a "culture war; where groups of people, usually of differing ages or stages whose musical tastes and preferences collide."[171] Even though the listening movement has the potential for creating a "culture war" it is, nonetheless, a healthy component of the Repertory with Roots pedagogy of engagement because it gives youth the opportunity to critique the artist's message and context.

To facilitate wise listening, the teacher provides a copy of the song lyrics for each participant. Also, integral to helping youth become wise listeners and hearers is providing opportunities to carefully and critically question the piece being studied. This can be achieved through the process of asking questions after listening to a song, spoken word, poem, etc. It is the responsibility of the session facilitators to immerse students in discussion about the music or poetry that engenders the use of meaning-making. Interpretive questions, which require students to make sense of information, are appropriate in this movement. [172] This means that listening has to be a central movement in all that is done in the pedagogy of engagement. Through listening we move youth toward answering key interpretive questions.

**Connecting** has to do with three specific meanings. First, it has to do with helping youth connect their stories with the biblical story in order for them to witness God's presence and action in their lives. Second, as a movement, music connects youth with their feelings and bodily expressions of meanings derived from listening to African American music. The intent is to connect youth with meanings of faith in God and Christian living. Third, as a movement, connecting refers to linking stories of empowerment in order to discover resources for daily living.

Connecting is associating one's experience with concepts explored in Black music by identifying relationships between the concepts and "real life" as a means of understanding self and others differently. It places the participant's life experiences in conversation with what has been heard and discussed. Because songs and poems are infused with new insights and meanings, connections between the artist's message and the student's life circumstances help stimulate the student's imagination. Thus, while examining the music, youth may form fresh and insightful approaches to the realities and challenges of their lives.

The use of questions is helpful in the movement of connecting because questions tend to open a new window of thought and to give persons an opportunity to voice their experiences. Questions can require students to think beyond specific information in the lesson.[173] They are integral to the connecting movement. Critical reflection calls forth the connecting movement as students share in large groups, small groups or pairs to communally engage in discussion. Connecting is essential in helping youth think of themselves as a part of the everyday story communicated in African American music, the larger story of God, and what these mean for the present and future.

**Engaging** employs a holistic model of learning wherein teachers and students grow, and are empowered by the learning process.[174] In the context of the Repertory with Roots pedagogy of engagement it also specifically includes wrestling, struggling or grappling. Engaging is socially, emotionally and spiritually wrestling with the subject matter that has been probed through systematic investigation in order to facilitate meaning making. "Nitty-gritty" hermeneutics also assists in defining this movement. A theological term coined by African American Religion Scholar Anthony Pinn, "nitty-gritty" hermeneutics is a model for understanding culture and theology. "Hermeneutics denotes interpretation of the meaning submerged in events, texts, etc. That is, words and texts contain valuable information that must be recognized and processed within one's system of values and concerns.[175] Engaging Black music gives youth the opportunity to wrestle via "nitty-gritty" hermeneutics with oppression, racism, and sexism in their own lives and social reality.

Social, emotional and spiritual forms of engaging generate different kinds of opportunities for meaning making. Social wrestling promotes sharing one's point of view and inviting others to agree or disagree. Emotional wrestling values cognitive dissonance, which is the feeling of uncomfortable tension which comes from holding two conflicting thoughts in mind at the same time. For a participant, this may prompt awareness that one's values are in opposition to the message they are hearing. This reality prods youth to examine and reexamine their points of view and share their experiences of conflict with the gathered community. Through exposure to the biblical text and God-centered stories or theological resources, students are better able to understand Christian values and how they affirm or contradict their own values. Spiritual wrestling includes looking for theological themes, biblical stories, Christian practices or echoes of other religious traditions as a part of meaning making.[176]

To facilitate the process of engaging, Wimberly's story-linking model enables youth to engage the biblical story with the everyday story. This is done by allowing students to share their own thoughts about the biblical story or theological concepts in light of what they have heard. It affords students the opportunity to look at biblical stories in a way that creates a foundation for Black youth in their journey toward wisdom formation. Through entering the biblical text as an integral component of Repertory with Roots pedagogy of engagement, youth become aware of what the scripture calls them to do as disciples.

Social, emotional and spiritual wrestling afford opportunities for the youth to grapple with hard issues found in Black music, history and culture and assess their value system in light of them. By engaging in these forms of wrestling, youth are made aware of God's work in their lives and in the lives of persons who are being examined. Engaging promotes awareness of God.

Asking evaluation questions are appropriate during the engaging movement. Evaluation questions push students to figure out why something happened, the result of an action, or how it could have been different.[177] Social, emotional and spiritual wrestling set up the fifth movement, "exploring."

**Exploring** includes a process of reading, gleaning and looking at writings, audio and video resources from the African American cultural, historical, literary or wisdom tradition. Exploring these writings with song lyrics bring forth new faith concepts and ideas. During this movement, the youth might read about people and events from African American Diasporic heritage. From these readings young can learn about the nature of relationships and life events. These readings show how African American heroes lived faithfully amidst historic events critical to African American heritage.

Looking at stories, quotations, and videos from the African American cultural, historical, literary or wisdom tradition is also a means of exploring possible new concepts and ideas that are integral to the African American youth's identity in American society. It is important to explore historical themes in African American heritage in the Repertory with Roots pedagogy of engagement because through exploration, youth are systematically exposed to the richness of their cultural tradition as African Diasporic people. Exploring the African American cultural, historical, literary and wisdom tradition honors the lives, spirit and culture of African Americans.

Application questions are important to this movement. Application questions allow students to think about how the subject matter might make a difference to them.[178] It helps learners to use what they know in their various life situations and contexts and discover the relevance of what they are learning and how to put it into practice in their lives.

**Emerging** involves the youth creating something new from the subject matter through embracing the content as a means of claiming identity. Emergence includes providing students with the opportunity to justify, expand and enrich their own process as thinkers, writers and composers. In the process of emerging, community members continue to feel like they belong to each other because they are hearing one another's voices, claiming ownership and expressing their personal and communal identity through their work.

Emerging further develops the youth's voice and encourages them to become collaborators with musical artists and one another in a creative process. Repertory with Roots is creative because it helps youth find voice and hope. Drawing from the aesthetics of Black music, the pedagogy seeks to incorporate creative ideas and creative experiences for African American youth. It reinforces the idea and ideal of a community's creative power. Emergence helps youth understand that they are capable of saying or creating something powerful. As peers in collaboration with one another, youth become aware of their similarities and differences.

To facilitate the emergence of something new from the subject matter, youth are asked to fashion their own artistic composition (rap, spoken word, drawing, portrait, song, journal entry, poem, brochure, story, etc.) to demonstrate their new relationship with the concepts they have encountered. Youth are not only commissioned to create but to share their artistic expressions as well. By sharing their creative work, youth hear each other's voices, inspiring a sense of community within the wisdom forming process.

**Honoring** involves in a closing ritual that respects participant's emerging understandings, meanings, voices and hopes. The ritualistic expression inspires a sense of community in the educational process that is directed toward wisdom formation.

A closing ritual honors the members of the gathered community by expressing gratitude for their participation in the teaching and learning experience. It calls attention once again to the goals studied. It invites moments of reflection by members of the community and ends with a communal blessing calling forth wisdom and hope among all. It is a ritual designed to emphasize communal belonging.

To guide the movement of honoring, youth are asked to participate in a ritual that brings closure to the teaching and learning experience. Components of a closing ritual might include songs, mediations, prayers, blessings and benedictions. At the end of the ritual extinguish the candle.

These seven movements comprise the Repertory with Roots pedagogy of engagement. This chapter has described components that are important to the pedagogical process. Learning styles and multiple intelligences identify the various ways that students learn. Asking great questions demonstrate the value of engaging students in discussion. Through pedagogical engagement, the seven movements afford teachers and participants an opportunity to engage faith, popular culture, African American history and culture in a systematic manner wherein each movement builds upon discussion, information and knowledge shared in the previous movement. In the appendices that follow chapter 10, we explore the Repertory with Roots pedagogy in action, focusing on the discipleship goals of belief formation, ethical embodiment, theological grounding, character development and historical-cultural enlightenment in five different experiential lessons.

## Chapter Ten

# Can I Get a Witness?—Experiential Lessons Introduced

*Every teacher teaches three lessons;*
*the one we plan to teach, the one we actually teach, the one we wish we had taught.*[179]

The guidelines in this chapter will help a teacher using the Repertory with Roots teaching and learning model to design a lesson plan that is as close to the third lesson as possible. This chapter will demonstrate the 'how-to's' of writing a Repertory with Roots lesson plan. It will contain key terms and definitions particular to this pedagogical approach to teaching and learning. Some ideas for consideration when planning a Repertory with Roots lesson will follow the lesson plan format. This chapter will end with a unit summary.

### Lesson Plan Terms and Definitions

**Title/Topic**—The lesson begins with the title of the lesson.

**Discipleship Goal**—Discipleship goals provide direction and define expected outcomes of discipleship education that focuses on Black youth, Black history, Black culture, Black music and the Bible. The five discipleship goals are defined and described in chapter 7. They are belief formation, ethical embodiment, theological grounding, character development and historical-cultural enlightenment.

**Time needed**—The suggested time is three sixty to seventy-five minute sessions. Session One movements include inviting, listening and connecting. Session Two movements include engaging and exploring. Session Three movements include emerging and honoring.

**Song—**-This section lists the song and the artist to be listened to during the session.

**Session Objectives**—An objective is a description of what learners should be able to learn/do during the lesson. Writing objectives is a three part process. First create a stem: *The participants will...*After creating a stem, add a verb that indicates what students will do. It might be helpful to secure a list of objective writing verbs from internet resources. *The participants will describe...*Once you have a stem and a verb, determine the actual process or outcome. *The participants will describe what it feels like to be excluded.* In the Repertory with Roots lesson plan format, usually one objective is written for each of the three sessions.

**Main Idea—**The main idea summarizes the point of the entire lesson. It communicates the most important thought to be explored during the lesson.

**Directions to the Session Leaders**—These instructions provide session leaders with recommendations on how to implement an orderly, creative and transformative teaching and learning experience.

**Set-Up**—This section describes how to prepare the learning environment and help participants to center themselves. Africentric cloth, a large jar candle and candle lighter is needed. When lighting the candle, words of centering such as "We light this candle as a symbol of God's love for us," describing the purpose for gathering is shared. Allow the candle to burn throughout the session. At the end of each session, extinguish the candle. Make sure that all materials and supplies are on hand for use during the session as well. Follow this set-up for each lesson.

**The Movements**—Review chapter 9 for a detailed description of each movement. Listed below is a brief summary of the movement's purpose and strategies for implementing it.

**Inviting**—Inviting summons the community to study. Opening ritual activities include reading quotations, meditations, litanies and prayers.

**Listening**—Listening calls the youth to hear the message in Black music and involves them in discussion about the meaning of the music. The following questions could be asked after listening: 1) What is the message of the song? 2) Why is this an important song to study? 3) How does this song connect with your life?

**Connecting**—Connecting helps youth identify commonalities and differences between their lives the song lyrics, the words of scripture and their feelings. The use of questions gives participants opportunities to give voice to their experiences.

**Engaging**—Engaging assists youth in wrestling with the subject matter in order to facilitate meaning making. During this movement, the Bible story or passage is introduced. To facilitate the process of engaging, the song lyrics and biblical text and personal experience are put into conversation with each other. Asking questions to decipher meaning is important as well as offering creative learning activities.

**Exploring**—Exploring guides youth in investigating African American historical and cultural resources that bring forth new concepts and ideas that potentially enrich and increase faith. Looking at stories, quotations, and movie clips from the Black tradition is a means of exploring possible new concepts and ideas that foster growth and development in African American youth's identity. Questions and hands-on activities are essential in this movement.

**Emerging**—Emerging encourages youth to create something new. Youth are asked to fashion their own artistic compositions (rap, poem, essay, prayer, portrait, tweet, spoken word, song, journal entry, brochure, drawing) to demonstrate their new relationship with concepts they have encountered during the lesson. Youth are not only commissioned to create but to share their expressions as well.

**Honoring**—Honoring admonishes youth to appreciate the knowledge gained. It includes a concluding activity that brings closure to the teaching and learning experience. Components of a closing ritual might include songs, meditations, prayers, blessings, affirmations, benedictions.

This lesson plan format outlines the lesson planning sequence for the Repertory with Roots Pedagogy of Engagement. What follows in Appendices A-E are five student-centered experiential lesson plans developed around each of the five discipleship goals—belief formation, ethical embodiment, theological grounding, character development, historical-cultural enlightenment.

## Some Ideas to Consider

The next section includes some thoughts about the rationale behind and successful execution of the teaching and learning sessions.

## Creativity

The first thought is to be creative. I have simply provided a lesson plan framework for your consideration; however I encourage you to think about your personal teaching style. Be imaginative. I cannot express that enough. Take liberty in crafting learning experiences that will work with your group. For example, do not feel constrained to complete every activity outlined in the lesson plan. As you feel the need, please revise or modify according to your needs and interests.

## Time

I am sure that you noticed that I did not prescribe a time frame for the various learning exercises. I did this purposely because every group is wired differently. Some groups thrive on discussion, others enjoy hands-on activity. Writing brings some groups to life, while others love to dig into the scriptures. With that being said, as a facilitator, you can determine what works best for your learning community. It is obvious that some activities will require more time than others. Feel free to shorten or lengthen as you feel necessary.

## Discussions

The majority of the lesson plans include several opportunities to engage in discussion or conversation. Feel free to shorten or lengthen discussion activity by not asking all questions or adding follow-up questions. Select the questions that you feel to be most important and achieve what you are trying to accomplish in the discussion. Add questions as you are led. Also, ask follow up questions as a measure to increase the effectiveness of your group discussion. They will also give young people the opportunity to clarify their thoughts. Finally, when leading discussions it is important to keep the discussion flowing freely, yet remaining on topic; encouraging continued conversation outside of the youth group.

## Suggested Answers

I have provided some suggested answers to various questions for points of explanation. However, the majority of the questions do not have responses provided. My goal in not providing all or the majority of the answers is because I wholeheartedly believe in participant exploration and engagement. So often in society, both youth and adults want the answers given to them. By providing the answers, the light of creativity is squelched and critical thinking skills are not developed. Questions in these lessons are for the most part open-ended, with a few factual questions included throughout. Hopefully, the questions will spark a desire to further explore the various topics of conversation.

## Materials/Supplies

Under each movement (inviting, listening, connecting, engaging, exploring, emerging, honoring) is a list of materials in parentheses to be used in the lessons. These lists identify the materials/supplies needed for each movement. Most materials include arts and crafts supplies, writing instruments, forms of paper, lesson handouts, song lyrics, DVD's, access to YouTube videos, CD/Digital music, screen, projector, journals, Africentric cloth, jar candle, candle lighter, Bibles. These materials/supplies assist in facilitating a meaningful, creative and transformative teaching session.

## Preparation

Teaching takes work. It has been my experience that a prepared teacher helps youth to engage in teaching and learning in ways that are meaningful for the whole community. Some lessons require that you not only gather materials, but prepare exhibits ahead of time. You may wish to view and listen to movies and music to become familiar with subject matter and theme. Be careful to read the lesson plans thoroughly and identify what preparation is needed to successfully facilitate the lesson plans. Not only is there preparation of lesson activities, but spiritual preparation is needed as well. Prayer and exploring the scriptures are critical to leading transformative learning experiences. Pray that the power of the Holy Spirit will grant you creativity and conviction as you facilitate and lead activities and discussions.

**Choosing Music/Media**—I'm sure the question you are asking is: "How do I choose music/media?" Honestly, I do not have a prescribed answer. I will affirm, "I love Black music in all its forms," see" Chapter 4. That is my starting point. Because I love Black music, I listen to Black music. Let that be your starting point as well. Begin to intentionally listen to various forms of Black music if you do not already do so. When you listen, listen with intentionally and a discerning ear to the lyrics for the messages in the music or media. Seek to discover the underlying worldview of the media piece. The worldview is the framework of beliefs through we view the world around us. When examining the worldview, pay attention to the content. Keep in mind that a Christian artist can present questionable content, and a non-Christian artist can write and create according to a Christian worldview. Exploration of the messages in the music/media is integral. Every time I hear a song/media piece or am drawn to a song/media piece, I approach it with intentionality. I ask myself the following questions: What lessons are embedded in this song/piece of media? How can I connect it with Black history, Black culture, and the Bible? What is the worldview? What are the music/media's theological viewpoints? What do I want youth to learn from engaging with this song/piece of media? These questions help me to choose music/media. It is also important to note that some Black music/media contains negative/counterproductive messages; these pieces can be explored as well. I strongly suggest that they are, use them to show how Black history, Black culture and the Bible do not support the claims of these pieces. Choosing music/media can be the most enjoyable aspect of creating Repertory with Roots lessons; it provides the opportunity to appreciate and enjoy the world of Black music on a whole new level.

These thoughts are offered as suggestions when creating and teaching the Repertory with Roots lesson plans. Remember to be creative, and use your time wisely to maximize your group's needs. Plan discussions; choose your questions based on your goals for discussion. Ask follow-up questions and stay on topic. Avoid rabbit trails. Encourage exploration, don't give all the answers. Gather materials/supplies before teaching. Prepare lesson exhibits, and prepare yourself spiritually by prayer and engaging the scriptures. Have fun and enjoy the ride.

**Unit Summary**

Chapters 9 and 10 have demonstrated the theory behind the construction of the Repertory with Roots pedagogy of engagement. The teaching model takes seriously the value of Black history, Black culture, Black music and the Bible in African American youth's identity formation. Before planning to teach, readers were encouraged to consider learning styles, multiple intelligences and the importance of asking great questions. The pedagogy's seven movements provide the scaffolding to frame this teaching model.

The fluidity of the movements—inviting, listening, connecting, engaging, exploring, emerging and honoring provide a trajectory for creating transformative learning experiences. To demonstrate creativity and originality, five student centered experiential lesson plans have been prepared for your use. Hopefully they will motivate you to create your own lesson plans particular to the needs and interests of your young people incorporating Black history, culture, music and the Bible. What you have witnessed are relational, real and relevant teaching and learning experiences for both youth and adults. These lessons affirm and confirm my sense that Black history, Black culture, Black music and the Bible have enormous potential for growth and change in the lives of African American youth.

# Conclusion

# When It's All Said and Done

*"When it's all been said and done*
*There is just one thing that matters*
*Did I do my best to live for truth?*
*Did I live my life for you?"*[180]

Writing Repertory with Roots: Black Youth, Black History, Black Culture, Black Music and the Bible has been a labor of love. My passion and interest in writing this work has spanned a period of more than ten years. Working and reworking, fashioning and refashioning, a pedagogical strategy for Christian education with African American youth has been formed. If you have ever visited the curriculum section in your local Christian bookstore, you will see very few youth ministry curriculum resources for Black youth by Black writers. This resource is my offering towards the effort of publishing more curriculum resources with Black youth in mind. When it's all said and done, I hope Repertory with Roots, accomplishes three things. First, I hope it stands for truth. Second, I hope it provides a new model for teaching that helps Black youth find voice and identity. Third, I hope it motivates youth leaders, pastors and others to begin creating curriculum materials that centers on the spiritual growth and development of Black youth.

## Stands for Truth

Repertory with Roots is not an ordinary model of Christian education for Black youth. It does not offer Bible study in a silo, but it is a model that integrates Black History, Black Culture and Black music and puts them in conversation with God's word. This cross-pollination provides a pathway toward Christian wisdom formation while engaging today's contemporary youth culture.

Contemporary youth culture is often cast in a negative light. The people, places, events, characters or ideas represented by contemporary youth culture are sometimes shunned or disregarded by Christians, the church or Christian organizations as the church struggles with what it looks like to be in the world and not of it. This is not a new problem. In 1951, theologian H. Richard Niebuhr wrote *Christ and Culture*. In that book he proposed that "Christ is the Transformer of Culture."[181] Niebuhr's view informs my understanding of Christ's interaction with culture and my conclusion that Repertory with Roots stands for truth. Niebuhr's position was centered on three truths. First, culture is an expression of God's good creation. It grows out of human creativity and community. Second, sin pollutes every part of creation, including culture. Third, culture can be redeemed or transformed in the name of Jesus Christ.[182] This redemption or transformation takes place when people seek to enhance and celebrate the "original good" found in a particular cultural object. The next step is to identify the effects of sin; the final step is to suggest ways to begin transforming aspects of the culture.

The task of introducing transformative elements to the fallen history, culture and music through the word of God is how "Repertory with Roots" stands for truth. It is not a perfect model, but it provides creative and engaging ways for Black youth to encounter Biblical truths with the roots and sources of their identity—Black history, Black culture and Black music.

**New Model for Teaching Black Youth to Find Voice and Identity**

At a recent youth group gathering, I asked the students to name their favorite songs. During the last few sessions of youth group, I began to feel that the Repertory with Roots model had fallen on deaf ears. Was Repertory with Roots making a difference? Are the youth even listening to and hearing what I am teaching? I was doubting myself, and I was doubting Repertory with Roots. I grabbed a pen and got ready to write the names of their favorite secular music artists and songs, but I was excitedly surprised by a response I did not anticipate.

As students identified their favorite song Carla raised her hand and said, "My favorite song is 'Worth'." I was startled. Not only because I wasn't expecting to hear it, but Carla remembered our very first session of the year, "I am Worth It." Five months after introducing the song, Carla was still claiming it as her anthem that is helping her to find voice and identity. Here is a sample of the lyrics:

"You thought I was worth saving
so, you came and changed my life.
You thought I was worth keeping
so you cleaned me up inside.

You thought I was to die for
so you sacrificed your life
so I could be free
so I could be whole
so I could tell everyone I know"[183]

Carla's declaration is a demonstration of the transforming power of the Holy Spirit working through the Repertory with Roots pedagogy of engagement. Carla has had struggles with issues of self-esteem and identity and "Worth" has provided a new way for her to identify herself in Christ. The historical, cultural, musical and biblical resources come together to help youth find their voice and their identity. Both voice and identity are necessary components for helping youth to affirm who and whose they are—unashamedly and unapologetically. For that reason, writing Repertory with Roots is worth the time and investment.

## Motivating Others to Create Curriculum Resources for African American Youth

My task and purpose for writing is not only to change student's lives, but to motivate youth leaders, and other youth advocates to write their own lessons. Writing curriculum is my passion, and I am sure that there are some of you who feel the same way. Repertory with Roots is my offering, my legacy to leave an imprint in the area of curriculum resources for Black youth. I encourage you to "write." Use the gift that God has given you. Share your lessons on life, learning and Biblical truth with Black youth. Begin with your local youth group. Black youth need creative, engaging and committed teachers to teach them the word of God in transformative ways. Black youth are living in a state of emergency. Peer pressure, violence, obsession with body image, low self-esteem, apathy, police brutality and stereotypical media messages are constant companions of today's Black youth. Black youth need God. Black youth need healthy relationships. Black youth need God's word shared in a language they can understand.

Gospel artist Yolanda Adams sings, "What About the Children?" It is a plea for persons to stand in the gap and care about young people. She sings: "What about the children, to ignore is so easy. So many innocent children will choose the wrong way. So what about the children? Remember when we were children. And if not for those who loved us and who cared enough to show us, where would we be today?"[184] Black youth deserve to see and experience curriculum materials and resources created and taught with them in mind. In closing, I ask you to remember the words of the prophet Jeremiah 29:11which says, "For surely I know the plans I have for you says the Lord. Plans for your welfare and not for harm. To give you a future with hope." God's plans for Black youth are good. Be encouraged to join God's advantageous plan by walking alongside them as curriculum writers and teachers to usher in God's future with hope.

# Appendices

# Appendix A

# "The Power Of Prayer"

**Discipleship Goal: Belief Formation**

Belief formation is having a head and heart knowledge of God, Jesus and the Holy Spirit which frames our Christian belief system. Engaging in a firsthand experience of God the Father, Jesus the Son, and the Holy Spirit holds potential for moving youth beyond knowing about the Trinity to actually knowing and being in relationship with the Trinity.

**Time Needed:** 3 sessions of 60-75 minutes.

**Song:** "Help!"—Erica Campbell featuring LeCrae

**Session Objectives:**

1. Participants will explore the message in the music about prayer and identify people, places and things that need God's Help.
2. Participants will describe events in Daniel 6, and identify lessons on prayer. They will write their own goals for their prayer time with God.
3. Participants will engage in prayer station activities that highlight the five parts of prayer—praise, thanksgiving, confession, petition and intercession.

**Main Idea:**

Life is not meant to be lived alone. We have been given a support system—God the Father, Jesus the Son, the Holy Spirit and our brothers and sisters in Christ. One way that we support each other is through prayer. Prayer is a form of life support. We need it to survive.

**Directions to the Session Leaders:**

Prior to teaching this lesson, please complete the following:

- Pray for direction, creativity and conviction.
- Read the entire lesson plan, including the leader notes—Daniel, Prayer Stations, Prayer Posters.
- Read the Bible passages identified.
- Listen to "Help"
- Watch the YouTube video, "Help-Erica Campbell Ft. LeCrae Lyrics" (4:09)
- Print song lyrics for each participant. Lyrics can be found at www.azlyrics.com or www.song-lyrics.com.
- Print lesson handouts for each participant. Handouts are located at the end of the lesson in order of use.
- Gather all session materials.
- Be open to the moving of the Holy Spirit during discussions, conversations and activities.

## SESSION ONE—THE POWER OF PRAYER

### SET-UP

**(You'll need an Afrocentric cloth, large jar candle, candle lighter)**

1. On a table place a piece of Afrocentric cloth and a large jar candle.
2. Begin by saying, "We light this candle as a symbol of the power of prayer."
3. Light the candle. Continue the session with "INVITING."

### INVITING

**(You'll need to make 5 signs label each one with the following sentence starters: 1) Lord, I confess...2) Lord, I praise you... 3) Lord, I thank you...4) Lord, I ask...5) Lord, I need...)**

1. Before the start of the session, post the signs in an area where participants can see, on the wall, on the floor. (Do not throw signs away, they will be used again during the movement—honoring)
2. Gather in a circle. Each person should offer a one sentence prayer using one of the following sentence starters:
   - Lord, I praise you ...
   - Lord, I confess...
   - Lord, I thank you...
   - Lord, I ask...
   - Lord, I need...
3. After each participant has offered a prayer, say, "Lord, hear our prayers."

### LISTENING

**(You'll need the CD/MP3 file—Help! By Erica Campbell featuring LeCrae or the YouTube video "Help-Erica Campbell Ft. LeCrae Lyrics" (4:09), and lyrics to Help! by Erica Campbell featuring LeCrae)**

1. Pass out lyrics to each participant.
2. Ask the participants to listen to what Erica and LeCrae are praying about. Circle those things on the lyrics page.
3. Play the song.
4. After listening, ask the following questions:
   - What is the message of this song?
   - Why do Erica and LeCrae need help?
   - What is the significance of needing help from the Lord?

## CONNECTING

**(You'll need paper, pens, and pencils)**

1. Pair the students together and ask them to share an experience when they needed the Lord's help. What did they do?
2. Have each participant create a list of people, places and things that need God's help. Have students keep their lists for later.
3. Ask a student to say a prayer to close the session.
4. Extinguish the candle.

## SESSION TWO—THE POWER OF PRAYER

### SET-UP

**(You'll need an Afrocentric cloth, large jar candle, candle lighter)**

1. On a table place a piece of Afrocentric cloth and a large jar candle.
2. Begin by saying, "We light this candle as a symbol of the power of prayer."
3. Light the candle continue the session with "ENGAGING."

### ENGAGING

**(You'll need Bibles, paper, markers, crayons, individual containers of molding clay/playdoh, journals, and the Thoughts for the Unapologetic Teenager Handout, p .114)**

**Leader Notes—Daniel:** Daniel's name means "God is my judge." From a study of his life, we can see that Daniel lived up to his name. Daniel was a Jew; a member of God's chosen people, the Israelites. He was sent to Babylon from Jerusalem to live in exile because the Israelite people were not faithful to God. However, Daniel was different. He was faithful to God in the midst of difficult circumstances. Because Daniel was so faithful, God used him to win the loyalty of kings and kingdoms.

One of the most popular stories of Daniel's faithfulness took place in Daniel 6, when Daniel was sentenced to spend the night in the lion's den because he continued to pray to the God of Israel when he was commanded not to. From Daniel we learn that prayer changes things, and that all of us need a little "Help" from God some time. Chapter 6 tells the story from beginning to end; his encounter with the king, administrators, high officers and the lions. As you read, think, what can I learn about prayer from Daniel's story.

1. Read the leader notes—Daniel, prior to the session. Share the following facts with the participants:
    - Daniel's name means "God is my judge."
    - Daniel was taken from his home land in Jerusalem to live in the foreign country, Babylon.
    - The Babylonians did not believe in the one true God.
    - Daniel's faith was challenged by living in Babylonian culture.
2. Ask, "Do any of you know anything about Daniel?"
3. Have students open their Bibles to Daniel 6. Allow students to read the story together in groups of three.
4. After reading, ask the following questions, allowing participants to find the answers in their Bibles.
    - What was Daniel's position in the kingdom? (vs. 1-3)
    - What words are used to describe Daniel? (vs. 4-5)
    - What did Daniel's haters try to do to destroy him? (vs. 6-9)
    - What did Daniel do after the decree had been published? (v. 10)
    - What was the consequence Daniel faced? (v. 16)

- How did God answer Daniel's prayer? (v. 22)
- What happened to Daniel's haters? (v. 24)
- What did King Darius write about God? (vs. 26-27)
- Describe Daniel's life after coming out of the lion's den. (v. 28)
- What lessons do you learn about prayer, faith and God's protection from this story?

5. Give students the opportunity to choose from the following art supplies—paper and markers, crayons to draw or molding clay to sculpt.
6. After students have gathered their supplies, pass out the Thoughts for Unapologetically Christian Teenager Handout
7. Follow up by saying, "Daniel shows us what it means to stand up for what you believe. He believed that God was his Judge and that God would save him no matter what. He talked to God through prayer. Prayer is our way to communicate with God also. What is your prayer life like? Think about it for a minute."
8. Read Thoughts for the Unapologetically Christian Teenager together.

**THOUGHTS FOR THE UNAPOLOGETICALLY CHRISTIAN TEENAGER**

"Help" from God in the life of an unapologetic Christian teenager leads to answered prayers. God loves you, just as he did Daniel. He wants you to have faith in Him, to trust Him and to believe that he will answer your prayers. **Draw** a picture of how God sees your relationship with him through prayer. What would the picture look like? If you could choose to show how God **molds/sculpts** you through prayer, what would the sculpture look like? If you could choose to describe how God parents you through prayer, would he be more like a father or a mother? **Elaborate**! In what other ways can you describe your prayer relationship with God? Draw, Sculpt/Mold, Write.

7. After drawing and sculpting, give students a few minutes to write in their journals.

**EXPLORING**

**(You'll need the Always Pray/Sojourner Truth Handout, page 115, S .M .A .R .T . Goals Handout, page 116, pens, pencils, and journals)**

1. Before teaching the lesson use Google Images to find a picture of Sojourner Truth to show to the group.
2. Pass out copies of Always Pray/Sojourner Truth Handout.
3. Read in pairs. Give students time to work through and write their responses.

**ALWAYS PRAY—SOJOURNER TRUTH**

Sojourner Truth was born in 1797 as Isabella, a Dutch speaking slave in New York. She was separated from her family at the age of nine years, and sold many times before she ended up at the Dumont plantation. She suffered physical and sexual abuse at the hands of her masters. Because she suffered so much, Sojourner loved to have conversations with God. She often went to the woods to spend time with the Lord. Her faith in prayer was equal to her faith in the love of Jesus. Sojourner said about prayer, "I believe in it and I shall pray. Thank God! Yes, I shall always pray." Sojourner often prayed out of her great pain. In 1851, she gave a speech, "Ain't I A Woman," at a Women's Convention in Akron, Ohio where she shared the suffering she had experienced as a mother. She says, "I have borne 13 children and seen most all of them sold off into slavery, and when I cried out with my mother's grief, none but Jesus heard me." Despite all that she went through, Sojourner never abandoned her faith in God.

- Where do you spend time with the Lord? Why this place?
- What causes you to pray? Explain.

Sojourner prayed consistently and with passion, especially about the return of her son. Read her prayer and feel her passion.

"Oh, God, you know how much I am distressed for I have told you again and again. Now help me get my son. If you were in trouble as I am, and I could help you, as you can help me, think I wouldn't do it? Yes, God you know I would do it. Oh, God, you know I have no money, but you can make the people do for me. I will never give you peace till you do, God. Oh, God, make the people hear me—don't let them turn me off, without hearing and helping me." (Conversations with God, 55)

- Comment on the tone of Sojourner's prayer. What do you think her relationship with God was like?
- What kind of attitude should we have towards prayer? See Philippians 4:6.
- Did Sojourner give up in prayer? How do you know?
- What are we instructed to do in prayer? See Luke 18:1.
- What are God's answers to prayer?
  - See 1 John 5: 14-15 (yes). See Psalm 40: 1 (wait). See James 1: 6-8 (no)
- Reflect on the song, the Bible story and the story/prayer of Sojourner Truth. What have you learned?
- How do you want your prayer life to change as a result of this session? Write in your journal.
- What are you going to do to improve your prayer life?

4. Gather the group together. Ask students to share key insights, perspectives and thoughts gained.

## Setting Goals for Prayer

1. Continue by saying, "Setting goals for our prayer time with God is one way to make prayer a priority and grow in our personal relationship with God. A S.M.A.R.T. goal can help with this."
2. Pass out copies of the S.M.A.R.T. Goals Handout. Read together.

## S.M.A.R.T. GOALS[185]

S=SPECIFIC— A specific goal has a much greater chance of being accomplished than a general goal.

- General Goal—I want to improve my prayer life.
- Specific Goal—I am going to write my prayers in my journal.

M=MEASURABLE—Measure your progress. Stay on track. Reach your target.

- I am going to write my prayers in my journal three days a week.

A=ACHIEVABLE—How can you make this goal come true?

- I am going to write my prayers in my journal three days a week before I go to bed at night.

R=REALISTIC—The goal you choose must work for you. Don't try to do too much. Be realistic.

- I am going to write my prayers in my journal three days a week before I go to bed at night, using the J.O.Y. model (Jesus, Others, You).

T=TIMELY=A goal should be grounded in a time frame.

- I am going to write my prayers in my journal three days a week before I go to bed at night, using the J.O.Y. model (Jesus, Others, You) for two weeks.

3. Encourage students to write one S.M.A.R.T. goal for prayer in their journals.
4. Play the song "Help" to signal the beginning and end of the goal writing process.
5. Allow time for sharing and affirmation.
6. Have participants take out their prayer lists and spend a few moments praying about the items on their lists.
7. Extinguish the candle.

## SESSION THREE—THE POWER OF PRAYER

### SET-UP

**(You'll need an Afrocentric cloth, large jar candle, candle lighter)**

1. On a table place a piece of Afrocentric cloth and a large jar candle.
2. Begin by saying, "We light this candle as a symbol of the power of prayer."
3. Light the candle. Continue the session with "EMERGING."

### EMERGING

**(You'll need pens, pencils, paper, journals, markers, magazines, glue sticks, scissors, and 11x14 poster boards)**

**Leader Notes—Prayer Stations**

Create 5 prayer stations/tables with each of the following topics and scriptures typed/written out on a sign. Post the signs on each table. Introduce students to the prayer stations by walking them through and briefly explaining each station. Emphasize that they will be reading God's word about various types of prayer, and that they are expected to respond to what they read. Prayer stations include:

A. PRAISE
- Read Hebrews 13:15.
- Write the message you receive from this verse and identify what you should do.
- In your journal, write a poem, spoken word, song or other creative writing piece that praises God.

B. CONFESSION
- Read Proverbs 28:13.
- Write the message you receive from these verses and identify what you should do.
- In your journal write a letter to God confessing thoughts, words and actions that do not please him.

C. THANKSGIVING
- Read Psalm 118:1.
- Write the message you receive from this verse, and identify what you should do.
- In your journal write a list of at least 10 people, places or things that you are thankful for. Pray and tell God why you are thankful for each one.

D. PETITION
- Read John 16: 23-24.
- Write the message you receive from these verses and identify what you should do.
- In your journal, write/illustrate a prayer about what you need God to do for you personally.

E. INTERCESSION
- Read 1 Timothy 2: 1-2.
- Write the message you receive from this verse and identify what you should do.
- Choose one person, place, or thing that you need to pray for. Silently pray for who/what needs God's help.

1. When the prayer session is over, call participants together and explain the final activity—Prayer Posters.

**Leader Notes—Prayer Posters**

Create a poster that will help you remember the five parts of prayer. Each of the five aspects (praise, confession, thanksgiving, intercession, and petition) should be represented on your poster in some fashion; as well as images that represent those aspects. Hang your poster on the wall next to your bed to help you to remember to pray at night before going to bed and in the morning when waking up.

1. Pass out poster boards, markers, pens, pencils, glue sticks, scissors, magazines.
2. Give participants the opportunity to be creative. At the close of the activity allow a few students to share.

**HONORING**

**(You'll need to use the signs from the INVITING movement: 1) Lord, I confess...2) Lord, I praise you... 3) Lord, I thank you...4) Lord, I ask...5) Lord, I need...)**

1. Gather in a circle. Each person should offer a one sentence prayer using one of the following sentence starters:
   - Lord, I praise...
   - Lord, I confess...
   - Lord, I thank you...
   - Lord, I ask...
   - Lord, I need...
2. After all prayers have been prayed, say, "Lord, hear our prayers."
3. Extinguish the candle.

# "The Power of Prayer" Handouts

## THOUGHTS FOR THE UNAPOLOGETICALLY CHRISTIAN TEENAGER

"Help" from God in the life of an unapologetic Christian teenager leads to answered prayers. God loves you, just as he did Daniel. He wants you to have faith in Him to trust Him and to believe that he will answer your prayers. **Draw** a picture of how God sees your relationship with him through prayer. What would the picture look like? If you could choose to show how God **molds/sculpts** you through prayer, what would the sculpture look like? If you could choose to describe how God parents you through prayer, would he be more like a father or a mother? **Elaborate**! In what other ways can you describe your prayer relationship with God? Draw, Sculpt/Mold, Write.

## ALWAYS PRAY SOJOURNER TRUTH

Sojourner Truth was born in 1797 as Isabella, a Dutch speaking slave in New York. She was separated from her family at the age of nine years, and sold many times before she ended up at the Dumont plantation. She suffered physical and sexual abuse at the hands of her masters. Because she suffered so much, Sojourner loved to have conversations with God. She often went to the woods to spend time with the Lord. Her faith in prayer was equal to her faith in the love of Jesus. Sojourner said about prayer, "I believe in it and I shall pray. Thank God! Yes, I shall always pray." Sojourner often prayed out of her great pain. In 1851, she gave a speech, "Ain't I A Woman," at a Women's Convention in Akron, Ohio where she shared the suffering she had experienced as a mother. She says, "I have borne 13 children and seen most all of them sold of into slavery, and when I cried out with my mother's grief, none but Jesus heard me." Despite all that she went through, Sojourner never abandoned her faith in God.

- Where do you spend time with the Lord? Why this place?

- Why do you pray? Explain.

Sojourner prayed consistently and with passion, especially about the return of her son. Read her prayer and feel her passion.

"Oh, God, you know how much I am distressed for I have told you again and again. Now help me get my son. If you were in trouble as I am, and I could help you, as you can help me, think I wouldn't do it? Yes, God you know I would do it. Oh, God, you know I have no money, but you can make the people do for me. I will never give you peace till you do, God. Oh, God, make the people hear me—don't let them turn me off, without hearing and helping me." (Conversations with God, 55)

- Comment on the tone of Sojourner's prayer. What do you think her relationship with God was like?
- What kind of attitude should we have towards prayer? See Philippians 4:6.
- Did Sojourner give up in prayer? How do you know?
- What are we instructed to do in prayer? See Luke 18:1.
- What are God's answers to prayer?
    - See 1 John 5: 14-15. See Psalm 40: 1. See James 1: 6-8.
- Reflect on the song, the Bible story and the story/prayer of Sojourner Truth. What have you learned?
- How do you want your prayer life to change as a result of this session? Write in your journal.
- What are you going to do to improve your prayer life?

## S.M.A.R.T. GOALS[186]

**S**=SPECIFIC— A specific goal has a much greater chance of being accomplished than a general goal.

General Goal—I want to improve my prayer life.

**Specific Goal—I am going to write my prayers in my journal.**

**M**=MEASURABLE—Measure your progress. Stay on track. Reach your target.

**I am going to write my prayers in my journal three days a week.**

**A**=ACHIEVABLE—How can you make this goal come true?

**I am going to write my prayers in my journal three days a week before I go to bed at night.**

**R**=REALISTIC—The goal you choose must work for you. Don't try to do too much. Be realistic.

**I am going to write my prayers in my journal three days a week before I go to bed at night, using the J.O.Y. model (Jesus, Others, You).**

**T**=TIMELY=A goal should be grounded in a time frame.

**I am going to write my prayers in my journal three days a week before I go to bed at night, using the J.O.Y. model (Jesus, Others, You) for two weeks.**

Write your own S.M.A.R.T. Goal

S________________________________________

M________________________________________

A________________________________________

R________________________________________

T________________________________________

# Appendix B

# "Life Matters"

**Discipleship Goal: Ethical Embodiment**

The goal of ethical embodiment involves ethical decision making which leads to a personification of what a person believes and why he/she should act on it. People are commanded to live by the Golden Rule (Matthew 7:12); this speaks to a person's humanity and application of the Christian faith.

**Time Needed:** 3 sessions of 60-75 minutes

**Song:** "Don't Shoot"—The Game featuring various artists

**Session Objectives:**

1. Participants will explore messages in the music about murder and frustration; connecting those messages with issues of personal responsibility and the work of justice.
2. Participants will encounter, engage and examine the biblical story of Rizpah as a catalyst that undergirds the activist work of Sybrina Fulton (mother of Trayvon Martin), Nicole Paultrie Bell (wife of Sean Bell), and Kadiatou Diallo (mother of Amadou Diallo).
3. Participants will prioritize societal issues that call for a justice response; identifying ways they can learn more about the issues and get involved.

**Main Idea:**

Life matters simply because it is a gift from God. Over the years we have seen many unarmed Black youth and adults murdered at the hands of law enforcement officials and others who did not see the value in their lives. This lesson honors and remembers those victims and their families. At the same time it celebrates the work of justice taking place in our communities and calls us to join that work by examining the connection between personal responsibility and justice.

**Directions to the Session Leaders:**

Prior to teaching this lesson, please complete the following:

- Pray for direction, creativity and conviction.
- Read the entire lesson plan including the leader notes—Rizpah—Story Backdrop, Creating a Wall of Remembrance, Lament
- Read the Bible passages identified.
- Listen to "Don't Shoot."
- Watch the YouTube video, "Don't Shoot Lyrics—The Game Ft. Various Artists" (6:04)
- Print song lyrics for each participant. Lyrics can be found at www.azlyrics.com or www.songlyrics.com.
- Print lesson handouts for each participant. Handouts are located at the end of the lesson in order of use.
- Gather all session materials.
- Be open to the moving of the Holy Spirit during discussions, conversations and activities.

## SESSION ONE—LIFE MATTERS

### SET-UP

**(You'll need an Afrocentric cloth, large jar candle, candle lighter)**

1. On a table, place a piece of Afrocentric cloth and a large jar candle.
2. Begin by saying: "We light this candle affirming that Life Matters."
3. Light the candle; continue the session with "INVITING."

### INVITING

**(You'll need copies of the Life Matters Litany Handout, p.95)**

1. Pass out copies of the Life Matters Litany.
2. Ask participants to stand.
3. Choose one participant to serve as the leader; the rest will serve as the group.
4. Read the litany responsively.

**Life Matters Litany**

Leader: Life begins with God. God has breathed into our bodies the breath of life.

Group: We believe and know that life matters.

Leader: Life begins with Jesus Christ. Because Jesus died for our sins and rose on the third day, we have new life if we believe on His name.

Group: Jesus, we believe and know that you give us new life through your blood.

Leader: The Holy Spirit sustains and keeps our life through His power and protection.

Group: Our life is empowered and protected through the promises of the Holy Spirit.

Everyone: Because of God, life matters. Because of Jesus Christ, life matters, Because of the Holy Spirit, life matters. Life is special and sacred because God the Father, God, the Son and God, the Holy Spirit created this gift. It is so!

5. After reading, sit down.

### LISTENING

**(You'll need the CD/MP3 file—"Don't Shoot" by The Game featuring Various Artist or the YouTube video "Don't Shoot Lyrics—The Game Ft. Various Artists" (6:04), and lyrics to "Don't Shoot.")**

1. Pass out the lyrics to each participant.
2. Ask the participants to listen for the obvious and not so obvious messages in the song. Obvious messages can be easily identified. (For example, saving our future, God ain't put us on the earth to get murdered). Not so obvious messages might be a little harder to identify. Think in terms

of what is the song really saying, or what is the underlying message? (Examples might include, Black bodies are disrespected—Mike Brown lying out in the cold, protests are not the solution to the problem)

3. Play the song.
4. After listening, ask the questions below. Encourage participants to refer to the lyrics as needed.
   - What is the message of "Don't Shoot?"
   - What are the obvious messages in the song?
   - What are some of the not so obvious messages?
   - What is the significance of the term "History keep repeating itself "(v. 2)? How does this term affect us today?
   - Why is killing teens synonymous with killing dreams (v. 1)?
   - Why is the lack of consequences for those who kill unarmed black youth and adults so frustrating?
   - What are some alternative solutions to rioting, looting and destroying our communities when unjust verdicts are given?

**CONNECTING**

**(You'll need the lyrics to "Don't Shoot", the Justice & Personal Responsibility Handout-p.96, pens, pencils and Bibles)**

1. Continue fostering the connection between the song and the participant's experiences by asking the following questions:
   - Read the Intro. What sticks out to you?
   - DJ Khaled says we should scream for justice? What is justice? (fairness, doing the right thing, equality)
   - Read the "Hook," God ain't put us on this earth to get murdered, its murder. Why did God put us on this earth?
   - How have you screamed for justice in your own life? What was the outcome? (Example: I stood up for a friend who was being bullied. I told an adult)
2. Pass out the Justice and Personal Responsibility Handout to each participant.
3. Complete Parts 1 & 2 as a group. Complete Part 3 independently. Answer the questions together in Part 4.

**Justice & Personal Responsibility**

Read through passages, answer the questions, complete the tasks.

**Part 1**

Read Micah 6: 8

- No, O people, the LORD has told you what is good and this is what he requires of you: to do what is right, to love mercy, and to walk humbly with your God. (NLT)

What is our personal responsibility according to Micah 6:8?

**Part 2**

Read Mark 12: 29-31

- 29 Jesus replied, "The most important commandment is this: 'Listen, O Israel! The LORD our God is the one and only LORD. 30 And you must love the LORD your God with all your heart, all your soul, all your mind, and all your strength.' 31 The second is equally important: 'Love your neighbor as yourself.' No other commandment is greater than these."

What three things does Jesus command us to do in these verses?

**Part 3**

Open your Bibles. Read Exodus 20: 1-17, and classify the 10 commandments. List each commandment that speaks about our relationship with God. List each commandment that speaks about our relationship with others. (Verses 2-11 relationship with God, Verses 12-17 relationship with others)

**Part 4**

- How are Micah 6:8, Mark 12: 29-31 and Exodus 20:1-17 connected to justice and personal responsibility?
- What injustices were mentioned in the song, "Don't Shoot?"
- When people do not live in personally responsible ways, it can lead to acts of injustice in our families, communities and world. Describe what can be done to encourage people to act in personally responsible ways.
- How will you live your life differently as a result of this session?

4. Before ending the lesson, gather in a circle, ask each participant to complete the following sentence- "A just society is..."
5. Extinguish the candle.

## SESSION TWO—LIFE MATTERS

### SET-UP

**(You'll need an Afrocentric cloth, large jar candle, candle lighter)**

1. On a table, place a piece of Afrocentric cloth and a large jar candle.
2. Begin by saying, "We light this candle affirming that Life Matters."
3. Light the candle; continue the session with "ENGAGING."

## ENGAGING

**(You'll need Bibles, the Rizpah Handout-p .133-134, Photos/Bios for Wall of Remembrance- p .135-136, pens, pencils and journals)**

1. Ask participants to turn in their Bibles to 2 Samuel 21: 1-14 to read the story of Rizpah.
2. Have participants read Round Robin Style, reading one verse per person around in a circle.
3. After reading, ask "What is the main idea?"
4. To facilitate a more in-depth understanding of the story, pass out copies of the Rizpah handout.
5. Choose five readers. Assign each one a paragraph to read.
6. After reading ask the questions on the bottom of the handout.

### Leader Notes—Rizpah—Story Backdrop—2 Samuel 21: 1-14

Rizpah whose name means "a hot stone," was King Saul's second wife. She had two sons by King Saul, Armoni and Mephibosheth. We find her story in 2 Samuel 21: 1-14. One day Rizpah was standing on a hill in Israel watching seven men being executed. Two of those men were her sons. Her sons were being murdered for their father, King Saul's crimes. They were killed and their bodies were left to rot on the hillside, even though the law said that they were to be buried by sunset.

Rizpah, suffering and sorrowful refused to leave the scene, and stayed by the bodies of her sons. She spread sackcloth (cloth used as a sign of mourning) on a rock, sat down and refused to move except for beating off the birds during the day and the wild animals at night. She kept this vigil for about six months. She stayed there until her sons received a proper burial.

### Why Were Her Sons Executed?

King Saul, father of Rizpah's two sons, committed sin against the Gibeonites, by murdering them and trying to destroy them as a people. A promise had been made by Joshua that the Gibeonites would live in peace in the land. King Saul broke the promise, and Israel was now suffering a famine (lack of food) for 3 years. For revenge, the Gibeonites asked King David for seven of Saul's male offspring. David surrendered Rizpah's 2 sons and 5 of Saul's grandsons. It was blood for blood.

**The Link Between Sin & Death**

Rizpah's sons died at the hands of violent men. She most likely understood the terrible link between sin (Saul) and death (her sons). One person's sin is like a cancer that spreads. Rizpah refused to hide her sorrow, suffering and grief. She lived out her pain in public. Rizpah gave meaning to her sons' deaths by making the entire nation of Israel face the evil of what happened.

**Rizpah who believes in Justice**

After a time, King David's heart was touched. After hearing about Rizpah's loyalty and courage, the king ordered that the remains of those who had been executed to be buried. Rizpah called attention to the cost of sin (the death of her sons). She had very few rights and very little power, but her persistent courage gave meaning to the death of her sons. It is a tragic story, but it is a story of unconditional love of a mother who believed in justice, (equality, doing the right thing, fairness) on behalf of her murdered sons.

- What has Rizpah experienced? Why?
- What is her response to the situation?
- Should her sons have been punished for their father's crimes? Explain.
- Rizpah's vigil probably lasted for about six months, what do you think she went through during that time? What kept her going?
- Would you consider Rizpah's courageous act an act of justice? Why was it so important to have a proper burial for her sons? Explain.
- "Don't Shoot," speaks of unarmed black youth and adults being murdered. Rizpah experienced the loss of her sons to violence. How do these stories affect us today, and how do we respond to them?

7. Prior to the session, create a "Wall of Remembrance" to remember unarmed Black youth and adults who were murdered by law enforcement officers or others who did not value their lives.

**Leader Notes—Creating a Wall of Remembrance**

Materials needed—poster-board or cardstock, glue sticks, scissors, bios/photos of victims, tape

**Prep Time—Bios/Photos**

In the Handout's section are brief biographies of Black youth that will comprise the wall of remembrance. Edit and/or duplicate these biographies to create posters for the wall.

Use Google Images to find photos of the following Black youth and adults—Emmett Louis Till, Kimani Gray, Kendrec McDade, Ervin Jefferson, Amadou Diallo, Patrick Dorismond, Timothy Stansbury, Jr. , Sean Bell, Trayvon Martin, Oscar Grant, Aiyana Jones, Michael Brown, Rekia Boyd, Eric Garner, Tamir Rice.

**Prep Time—Creating Posters**

Create a poster for each victim. Use a piece of poster-board or cardstock. Glue the photo and corresponding bio to a piece of poster-board or cardstock.

**Setting Up—Wall of Remembrance**

After completing the posters, tape each one to the wall creating a wall of remembrance. Complete set up before the session.

8. After reading the story of Rizpah, call participants attention to the Wall of Remembrance. Read the following directions.

**Wall of Remembrance**

Posted around the room are posters of unarmed African American youth and adults who died violently. Please read each person's story. If you feel moved, write a memorial note on the poster. Please walk and read in silence.

9. After paying respect to the victims, have participants return to their seats.
10. Encourage participants to take out their journals and respond to the following writing prompt.

**Writing Prompt**

Reflect on "Don't Shoot," Micah 6:8, Mark 12: 29-31, Exodus 20: 1-17, the story of Rizpah and the Justice and Personal Responsibility Handout. How do these stories, songs and Bible verses serve as evidence that life matters? Write a life matters statement that affirms what you believe about God, justice and personal responsibility.

**EXPLORING**

**(You'll need the Rizpah's Legacy Handout-p .137, photos of Sybrina Fulton, Nicole Paultrie Bell, Kadiatou Diallo, pens, pencils)**

1. Prior to the session, use Google images to find and print photos of Sybrina Fulton (mother of Trayvon Martin), Nicole Paultrie Bell (wife of Sean Bell), and Kadiatou Diallo (mother of Amadou Diallo).
2. Pass out Rizpah's Legacy Handout. Show pictures of the three women.
3. Choose three participants to read each story.
4. After reading, ask the questions at the bottom of the page.

**Rizpah's Legacy**

**Mom's on a Mission...Turning Pain Into Action**

**SYBRINA FULTON**, mother of Trayvon Martin, 14, is a mom on a mission, turning her pain into action. She is unyielding in her pursuit of justice for her slain son. We call her a Daughter of Rizpah. She is working to build the Trayvon Martin Foundation whose mission is to promote a just, violence free society by expanding the organization's programs to other cities and towns across the country. Initiatives such as the Peace Walk and Peace Talk bring together young people, community leaders, law makers and law enforcement to help foster more equitable relations between police officers and the communities they serve. Ms. Fulton is also a part of Florida's coalition of legislators, law enforcement officials and citizens seeking to repeal the "Stand Your Ground" law, which allows those who believe they are being physically threatened to protect themselves with deadly force. Such laws exist in 22 other states.

**NICOLE PAULTRE BELL** was the fiancé of Sean Bell, 23, and mother of his two daughters. Sean died as a result of 50 bullets shot outside of a night club on the eve of the couple's wedding day. Nicole is on a mission, turning her pain into action. She is the founder and president of "When It's Real, It's Forever" (WIRIF), a justice and youth focused organization. WIRIF aims to reduce incidences of tragic encounters between innocent people and the police; to inform all citizens of their rights regarding police interaction and the legal system; and to promote positive youth development through sports leagues, music and other cultural arts programs. Nicole, a Daughter of Rizpah, fighting for justice for her daughters' father.

**KADIATOU DIALLO** is the mother of Amadou Diallo who was killed in a firestorm of 41 bullets fired by NYPD officers as he stood in the hallway of his apartment building. She supports the New York City based Diallo Foundation and the CADITEC—Amadou Diallo Technical Center for Computer Literacy, which she is established in Labe, Guinea for promoting educational opportunities for Africans and African Americans. The mission of her foundation is to ensure that students from the African Diaspora have access to a college education. She also tries to be present for other families who have faced similar circumstances such as hers.

- How are these mothers carrying on the Legacy of Rizpah?
- How has turning their pain into action helped the cause of humanity?
- How do their lives incorporate justice and personal responsibility in their work?
- As we think about the need for justice and fairness in our world, what thoughts are you having about helping the cause of humanity?

5. Prior to ending the session, ask each participant to complete the following sentence, "Life matters because..."
6. Extinguish the candle.

## SESSION THREE—LIFE MATTERS

### SET-UP

**(You'll need an Afrocentric cloth, large jar candle, candle lighter)**

1. On a table, place a piece of Afrocentric cloth and a large jar candle.
2. Begin by saying, "We light this candle affirming that Life Matters."
3. Light the candle; continue the session with "EMERGING."

## EMERGING

**(You'll need the We Believe Life Matters Handout-p.138, pens, pencils, and journals)**

1. Read the quotes from Micah 6:8 and Civil Rights Activist Ella Baker.
   - "No, O people, the LORD has told you what is good and this is what he requires of you: to do what is right, to love mercy, and to walk humbly with your God.'(NLT)
     ~Micah 6:8
   - "The struggle is eternal. The tribe increases. Somebody else carries on."
     ~Ella Baker

2. How are these two quotes related to each other?
3. Pass out the handout, We Believe Life Matters.
4. Read the directions with the group.

### WE BELIEVE LIFE MATTERS

**Directions**

In a group of 3-4 students, brainstorm what you believe to be the most crucial issues that we face in the world today. After identifying your issues, in the first column, come up with a number of how important the issue is, 5 being the highest. In the second column, write a number for how much you know about the topic. In the third column, identify how you can learn more and get involved.

| | Issues | 0-5 | 0-5 | Learning More Getting Involved |
|---|---|---|---|---|
| 1 | | | | |
| 2 | | | | |
| 3 | | | | |
| 4 | | | | |

**Journaling—Write all About It**

- Why did you choose these issues? Why are they significant?
- What are you going to do to learn more about one of these issues?
- What can you do about this issue that will make a difference?
- What is your plan for learning more and getting involved?
- Write a prayer in your journal about your response to what we've experienced in the sessions, Life Matters.

**HONORING**
**(You'll need the Leader Notes on Lament, Bibles)**

1. Read the leader notes on Lament to participants.

**Leader Notes—LAMENT**—A lament or complaint is an expression of sorrow or grief. Psalm 13 is an example. It begins with despair, but ends in optimism, because there is always hope in God. The senseless killing of unarmed Black youth and adults has and continues to be a source of grief and sorrow in our communities. Today, we cry out to God. God sees our tears. He hears our cries. He knows our pain. God is a mender of broken hearts and a healer of wounded spirits. As we work for justice, God will restore our joy. Today we pray on behalf of our slain brothers and sisters, their families and our communities. We pray for the work of justice. Let it begin with us. Lord, hear our prayer, and we say...O' Lord how long...

2. Continue by reading Psalm 13 together.
3. Extinguish the candle.

# "Life Matters" Handouts

## Life Matters Litany

Leader: Life begins with God. God has breathed into our bodies the breath of life.

Group: We believe and know that life matters.

Leader: Life begins with Jesus Christ. Because Jesus died for our sins and rose on the third day, we have new life if we believe on His name.

Group: Jesus, we believe and know that you give us new life through your blood.

Leader: The Holy Spirit sustains and keeps our life through His power and protection.

Group: Our life is empowered and protected through the promises of the Holy Spirit.

Everyone: Because of God, life matters. Because of Jesus Christ, life matters, Because of the Holy Spirit, life matters. Life is special and sacred because God the Father, God the Son and God the Holy Spirit created this gift. It is so!

## Justice & Personal Responsibility

Read through the passages, answer the questions. Complete the tasks.

**Part 1**—Read Micah 6: 8

- No, O people, the LORD has told you what is good and this is what he requires of you: to do what is right, to love mercy, and to walk humbly with your God. (NLT)

What is our personal responsibility according to Micah 6:8?

**Part 2**—Read Mark 12: 29-31

- 29 Jesus replied, "The most important commandment is this: 'Listen, O Israel! The LORD our God is the one and only LORD. 30 And you must love the LORD your God with all your heart, all your soul, all your mind, and all your strength.' 31 The second is equally important: 'Love your neighbor as yourself.' No other commandment is greater than these."

What three things does Jesus command us to do in these verses?

**Part 3**—Open your Bibles. Read Exodus 20: 1-17, and classify the 10 commandments. List each commandment that speaks about our relationship with God. List each commandment that speaks about our relationship with others.

God:

Others:

**Part 4**

- How are Micah 6:8, Mark 12: 29-31 and Exodus 20:1-17 connected to justice and personal responsibility?
- When people do not live in personally responsible ways, it can lead to acts of injustice in our families, communities and world. Describe what can be done to encourage people to act in personally responsible ways.
- How will you live your life differently as a result of this session?

## ~RIZPAH~

### Story Backdrop—2 Samuel 21: 1-14

Rizpah whose name means "a hot stone," was King Saul's second wife. She had two sons by King Saul, Armoni and Mephibosheth. We find her story in 2 Samuel 21: 1-14. One day Rizpah was standing on a hill in Israel watching seven men being executed. Two of those men were her sons. Her sons were being murdered for their father, King Saul's crimes. They were killed and their bodies were left to rot on the hillside, even though the law said that they were to be buried by sunset.

Rizpah, suffering and sorrowful refused to leave the scene, and stayed by the bodies of her sons. She spread sackcloth (cloth used as a sign of mourning) on a rock, sat down and refused to move except for beating off the birds during the day and the wild animals at night. She kept this vigil for about six months. She stayed there until her sons received a proper burial.

### Why Were Her Sons Executed?

King Saul, father of Rizpah's two sons, committed sin against the Gibeonites, by murdering them and trying to destroy them as a people. A promise had been made by Joshua that the Gibeonites would live in peace in the land. King Saul broke the promise, and Israel was now suffering a famine (lack of food) for 3 years. For revenge, the Gibeonites asked King David for seven of Saul's male offspring. David surrendered Rizpah's 2 sons and 5 of Saul's grandsons. It was blood for blood.

### The Link Between Sin & Death

Rizpah's sons died at the hands of violent men. She most likely understood the terrible link between sin (Saul) and death (her sons). One person's sin is like a cancer that spreads. Rizpah refused to hide her sorrow, suffering and grief. She lived out her pain in public. Rizpah gave meaning to her sons' deaths by making the entire nation of Israel face the evil of what happened.

### Rizpah who believes in Justice

After a time, King David's heart was touched. After hearing about Rizpah's loyalty and courage, the king ordered that the remains of those who had been executed to be buried. Rizpah called attention to the cost of sin (the death of her sons). She had very few rights and very little power, but her persistent courage gave meaning to the death of her sons. It is a tragic story, but it is a story of unconditional love of a mother who believed in justice, (equality, doing the right thing, fairness) on behalf of her murdered sons.

- What has Rizpah experienced? Why?
- What is her response to the situation?
- Should her sons have been punished for their father's crimes? Explain.

- Rizpah's vigil probably lasted for about six months, what do you think she went through during that time? What kept her going?
- Would you consider Rizpah's courageous act an act of justice? Why was it so important to have a proper burial for her sons? Explain.
- "Don't Shoot," speaks of unarmed black youth and adults being murdered. Rizpah experienced the loss of her sons to violence. How do these stories affect us today, and how do we respond to them?

## "WALL OF REMEMBRANCE BIOS"

**EMMETT LOUIS TILL,** (July 25, 1941 – August 28, 1955) was an African-American teenager who was murdered in Mississippi at the age of 14 after reportedly flirting with a white woman. Till was from Chicago, Illinois, visiting his relatives in Money, Mississippi. They took Till away to a barn, where they beat him and gouged out one of his eyes, before shooting him through the head and disposing of his body in the Tallahatchie River, weighting it with a 70-pound (32 kg) cotton gin fan tied around his neck with barbed wire. Three days later, Till's body was discovered and retrieved from the river.

**KIMANI GRAY,** Sixteen-year-old Kimani was shot four times in the front and side of his body and three times in the back by two New York City police officers as he left a friend's birthday party in Brooklyn on March 9, 2013. Kimani was empty handed when he was gunned down.

**KENDREC MCDADE**, Nineteen-year-old college student Kendrec McDade was shot and killed in March 2012 when officers responded to a report of an armed robbery of a man in Pasadena, Calif. He was later found to be unarmed, with only a cellphone in his pocket.

**ERVIN JEFFERSON**, The 18-year-old was shot and killed by two security guards outside his Atlanta home on Saturday, March 24, 2012. His mother says that he was unarmed and trying to protect his sister from a crowd that was threatening her.

**AMADOU DIALLO**, In 1999, four officers in street clothes approached Diallo, a West African immigrant with no criminal record, on the stoop of his New York City building, firing 41 shots and striking him 19 times as he tried to escape. They said they thought the 23-year-old had a gun. It was a wallet.

**PATRICK DORISMOND**, The 26-year-old father of two young girls was shot to death in 2000 during a confrontation with undercover police officers who asked him where they could purchase drugs.

**TIMOTHY STANSBURY JR.**, Unarmed and with no criminal record, 19-year-old Stansbury was killed in 2004 in a Brooklyn, N.Y. stairwell. The officer who shot him said he was startled and fired by mistake.

**SEAN BELL**, In the early-morning hours of what was supposed to be 23-year-old Bell's wedding day; police fired more than 50 bullets at a car carrying him and his friends outside a Queens, N.Y., strip club in 2006. Bell was killed, and two of his friends were wounded.

**TRAYVON MARTIN,** Was a 17-year-old African American from Miami Gardens, Florida who was fatally shot by George Zimmerman, a neighborhood watch volunteer, in Sanford, Florida. On the evening of February 26, Martin went to a convenience store and purchased candy and juice. As Martin returned from the store, Zimmerman spotted him and called the Sanford Police to report him, saying he looked suspicious. Moments later, there was an altercation between the two individuals in which Martin, who was unarmed, was shot in the chest.

**OSCAR GRANT**, Oscar Grant III was fatally shot by BART Police officer Johannes Mehserle in Oakland, California, in the early morning hours of New Year's Day 2009. Grant was unarmed; he was pronounced dead the next morning at Highland Hospital in Oakland.

**AIYANA JONES** was a seven-year-old African-American girl from the east side of Detroit, Michigan who was shot and killed during a raid conducted by the Detroit Police Department's Special Response Team on May 16, 2010· Her death drew national media attention and led U.S. Representative John Conyers to ask U.S. Attorney General Eric Holder for a federal investigation into the incident. Officer Joseph Weekley was charged in connection with Jones' death. In October 2011, Weekley was charged with involuntary manslaughter and reckless endangerment with a gun.

**MICHAEL BROWN,** The shooting of Michael Brown occurred on August 9, 2014, in Ferguson, a suburb of St. Louis County, Missouri. Brown, an 18-year-old black man, was fatally shot by Darren Wilson, 28, a white police officer of the Ferguson Police Department.

**REKIA BOYD,** A 22 year old African American woman, Rekia Boyd was shot and killed in March 2012 during a confrontation with an off-duty Chicago cop.

**ERIC GARNER**—On July 17, 2014, Eric Garner died in Staten Island, New York City, after a police officer put him in what has been described as a "chokehold" for about 15 to 19 seconds during an arrest.

**TAMIR RICE**— The shooting of Tamir Rice, a 12-year-old boy occurred on November 22, 2014, in Cleveland, Ohio. Two police officers responded after receiving a police dispatch call "of a male black sitting on a swing and pointing a gun at people" in a city park. A caller reported that a male was pointing "a pistol" at random people in the Cudell Recreation Center. The officers reported that upon their arrival, Rice reached towards a gun in his waistband. Within two seconds of arriving on the scene, the officer fired two shots hitting Rice once in the torso. Neither officer administered any first aid to Rice after the shooting. He died on the following day..

## Rizpah's Legacy

### Mom's on a Mission…Turning Pain into Action

**SYBRINA FULTON**, mother of Trayvon Martin, 14, is a mom on a mission, turning her pain into action. She is unyielding in her pursuit of justice for her slain son. We call her a Daughter of Rizpah. She is working to build the Trayvon Martin Foundation whose mission is to promote a just, violence free society by expanding the organization's programs to other cities and towns across the country. Initiatives such as the Peace Walk and Peace Talk bring together young people, community leaders, law makers and law enforcement to help foster more equitable relations between police officers and the communities they serve. Ms. Fulton is also a part of Florida's coalition of legislators, law enforcement officials and citizens seeking to repeal the "Stand Your Ground" law, which allows those who believe they are being physically threatened to protect themselves with deadly force. Such laws exist in 22 other states.

**NICOLE PAULTRE BELL** was the fiancé of Sean Bell, 23, and mother of his two daughters. Sean died as a result of 50 bullets shot outside of a night club on the eve of the couple's wedding day. Nicole is on a mission, turning her pain into action. She is the founder and president of "When It's Real, It's Forever" (WIRIF), a justice and youth focused organization. WIRIF aims to reduce incidences of tragic encounters between innocent people and the police; to inform all citizens of their rights regarding police interaction and the legal system; and to promote positive youth development through sports leagues, music and other cultural arts programs. Nicole, a Daughter of Rizpah, fighting for justice for her daughters' father.

**KADIATOU DIALLO** is the mother of Amadou Diallo who was killed in a firestorm of 41 bullets fired by NYPD officers as he stood in the hallway of his apartment building. She supports the New York City based Diallo Foundation and the CADITEC—Amadou Diallo Technical Center for Computer Literacy, which she is established in Labe, Guinea for promoting educational opportunities for Africans and African Americans. The mission of her foundation is to ensure that students from the African Diaspora have access to a college education. She also tries to be present for other families who have faced similar circumstances such as hers.

- How are these mother's carrying on the Legacy of Rizpah?
- How has turning their pain into action helped the cause of humanity?
- How do their lives incorporate justice and personal responsibility in their work?
- As we think about the need for justice and fairness in our world, what thoughts are you having about helping the cause of humanity?

## WE BELIEVE LIFE MATTERS

**Directions**

In a group of 3-4 students, brainstorm what you believe to be the most crucial issues that we face in the world today. After identifying your issues, in the first column, come up with a number of how important the issue is, 5 being the highest. In the second column, write a number for how much you know about the topic. In the third column, identify how you can learn more and get involved.

| | Issues | 0-5 | 0-5 | Learning More Getting Involved |
|---|---|---|---|---|
| 1 | | | | |
| 2 | | | | |
| 3 | | | | |
| 4 | | | | |
| 5 | | | | |
| 6 | | | | |
| 7 | | | | |

**Journaling—Write all About It**

- Why did you choose these issues? Why are they significant?
- What are you going to do to learn more about one of these issues?
- What can you do about this issue that will make a difference?
- What is your plan for learning more and getting involved?
- Write a prayer in your journal about your response to what we've experienced in the sessions, Life Matters.

# Appendix C

# "All About That Grace"

**Discipleship Goal:**

**Theological Grounding—**Theological grounding helps youth to develop a framework that helps them to understand the relationship between God, themselves, humanity and all of creation.

**Time Needed:** 3 sessions of 60-75 minutes

**Song:** "Take Me As I am"—LeCrae

**Session Objectives:**

1. Participants will explore the message in the music by analyzing the lyrics and identifying the connection between the lost and found.
2. Participants will compare/contrast the concepts of grace (prevenient, justifying, sanctifying) and mercy, and identify how these concepts are operative in their own life.
3. Participants will write a prayer of confession, acknowledging the grace and mercy of God by recognizing what it means to be lost.

**Main Idea:**

The Christian life if full of twists and turns, ups and downs, however, as we journey we never run out of grace. If we pay attention, we can witness God's grace in three distinct ways. First, there is prevenient grace; which is described as God's love and favor that actively seeks us. In other words, grace is chasing us down pursuing a relationship with us. Second, there is justifying grace; this involves us turning away from sin and entering into a relationship with God through Jesus Christ. Third, there is sanctifying grace.

Sanctifying grace moves us toward Jesus Christ and helps us to become more like him. As we look at our lives, we can see grace at work in many ways. Our lives as Christ followers is all about that grace.

**Directions to the Session Leaders:**

Prior to teaching this lesson, please complete the following:

- Pray for direction, creativity and conviction.
- Read the entire lesson plan, including the leader notes—Lost & Found, Parables, and the Lost Child Demonstration.
- Read the Bible passages identified.
- Listen to "Take Me As I Am."
- Watch the YouTube video, "Take Me As I Am—LeCrae (w/lyrics)" (4:47)
- Practice the Lost Child Demonstration.
- Print song lyrics for each participant. Lyrics can be found at www.azlyrics.com or www.song-lyrics.com.
- Read and become familiar with the handout, "Saved, Now Saved for Real."
- Print lesson handouts for each participant. Handouts are located at the end of the lesson in order of use.
- Gather all session materials.
- Be open to the moving of the Holy Spirit during discussions, conversations and activities.

## SESSION ONE—ALL ABOUT THAT GRACE

**SET-UP:**

**(You'll need an Afrocentric cloth, large jar candle, candle lighter)**

4. On a table, place a piece of Afrocentric cloth and a large jar candle.
5. Begin by saying: "We light this candle as a symbol of God's grace in our lives."
6. Light the candle; continue the session with "INVITING."

**INVITING**

**(You'll need the Looking to Jesus Handout, p. 154)**

1. Distribute the Looking to Jesus handout to each participant. Lead participants in reading and responding.

**Looking to Jesus**

"I met a man named Jesus, and I've had an exchange with him. I gave him my sorrows, he gave me his joy; I gave him my confusion, he gave me his peace; I gave him my despair, he gave me his hope; I gave him my hatred, he gave me his love; I gave him my torn life, he gave me his purpose."
(Rev. Otis Moss)

Leader: What did you give Jesus? What did he give you in return?

Group: Ask each person to respond individually to the two questions.

**Let Us Pray (All together)**

Jesus, our savior, we come. Jesus, our healer, we come. Jesus, our deliverer, we come.
We come wanting a closer relationship with you.
Lord, prepare our minds to understand your word.
Lord, prepare our hearts to receive your word.
Lord, prepare us to be living examples of your love in our lives.
In Jesus name, Amen.

## LISTENING

**(You'll need the CD/MP3 file—"Take Me As I Am" by LeCrae, or YouTube video "Take Me As I Am—LeCrae (w/lyrics)" (4:47), and the lyrics to "Take Me As I Am" by LeCrae)**

1. Pass out lyrics to each participant.
2. Play the song. Ask participants to read the lyrics as they listen.

3. After listening, ask the following questions:
   - What is LeCrae's message to his listeners?
   - What is the significance of the title, "Take Me as I Am?"
   - What did you learn about Jesus from this song? What did Jesus do?

**CONNECTING**

**(You'll need a $5 bill or other prize to hide)**

1. Have participants respond to the following questions in small groups of 3-4 persons.
   - What do you like about this song? Explain.
   - How does the song make you feel? Explain.
   - How does the message of "Take Me as I Am" relate to being lost?

**Leader Notes—Lost and Found**

You will need one five-dollar bill or other prize. Before the youth arrive, hide the five-dollar bill or other prize somewhere in the area. Make it hard to find, but not impossible. Explain that somewhere in this room is a five-dollar bill or prize. It has been lost. Whoever finds it may keep it. You have five minutes to find it. Watch the youth as they search for the prize. If time allows, discuss the following:

- Describe how you felt during the search.
- How did you feel as the winner? How did you feel as the loser?
- How does this activity connect to Jesus? Explain.
- How do you think Jesus feels when he finds us?
- Why do we sometimes play hard to find when Jesus looks for us?

2. Ask a student to say a prayer ending the session.
3. Extinguish the candle.

## SESSION TWO—ALL ABOUT THAT GRACE

### SET-UP:

**(You'll need a Afrocentric cloth, large jar candle, candle lighter)**

1. On a table, place a piece of Afrocentric cloth and a large jar candle.
2. Begin by saying: "We light this candle as a symbol of God's grace in our lives."
3. Light the candle; continue the session with "ENGAGING."

### ENGAGING

**(You'll need Bibles and the Lost Hoping to Be Found Handout, p .155)**

**Leader Notes—Parables: A Quick Synopsis**

Parables are stories Jesus frequently used when he was teaching. Parables have one central point. Teach one truth. To correctly interpret the parable, determine why the parable was told. Look for the intended meaning of the parable. Don't make up a meaning that's not clearly stated. Identify the central idea.

1. Read the leader notes Parables: A Quick Synopsis prior to the session. Share the following key points with the participants.
    - Parables are stories that have one central point.
    - Parables teach one truth.
    - As you listen, look for the meaning of the parable.
    - Identify the central idea.
2. Ask the participants, what are some parables Jesus told? (Weeds—Matthew 13: 24-30; Mustard Seed/Yeast—Matthew 13: 31-35; Sower—Mark 4: 1-9; Rich Fool—Luke 12: 13-21; Lost Sheep—Luke 15: 1-7; Lost Coin—Luke 15: 8-10)
3. Have students open their Bibles to Luke 15.
4. Give the students 3-5 minutes to read the entire chapter, but paying special attention to verses 11-32, The Parable of the Lost Son.
5. After reading silently, ask for five volunteers to read the story out loud.
    - Reader 1 (1-7)
    - Reader 2 (8-10)
    - Reader 3 (11-16)
    - Reader 4 (17-21)
    - Reader 5 (22-32)
6. After reading the parable, ask the following questions. Help students to discover the answers by looking at the verses listed.
    - Read verse 1, who was coming to Jesus?
    - Who was complaining and why were they complaining? (2)

- Review the parable of the lost son. Who are the main characters? (11)
- What is the story about?
- Where is the story taking place? (12-13)
- What did the younger son do after he left home? (13-15)
- What does "he came to his senses" mean?
- When the younger son realized he had nothing left, what did he do? (18)
- How did the father respond? (22-24)
- Where was the older son? (25)
- Why did he come home? (25)
- Why was there music and dancing? (26-27)
- How did the older brother feel about his younger brother's return? (28)
- How would you have felt? Explain.
- Why was the older brother angry? (29-30)
- How did the father respond to the older son's anger? (31-32)
- Who does the father represent in this story?
- Which characters represent each of us? Explain.

7. Ask, what is grace? What is mercy?
8. After participants respond, read the definitions for grace and mercy. Ask the corresponding questions.

This story/parable is an example of God's grace and mercy in action.

**Grace**—Blessings we receive that we cannot earn and do not deserve.

- What happened in the story that demonstrates God's grace?
- What has happened in your own life that demonstrates God's grace?

**Mercy**—When we don't receive the penalty or consequences of our sin that we deserve.

- What happened in the story that demonstrates God's mercy?
- What has happened in your own life that demonstrates God's mercy?

9. Distribute copies of the case study, "Lost Hoping to Be Found."
10. Read the case study in pairs.
11. Select 3 participants to role play the case study (Clarissa, Jamie, Narrator). After the role play, ask the questions and the end.

**Case Study—Lost Hoping to Be Found**

Clarissa was sitting on the hood of her boo Tyrone's car outside of the community center. Her cousin Jamie walked up to her and said, "What's up girl?"

Clarissa, said "Well, if it ain't Bible Girl, whatchu you doing down here with us heathens? This is where all the sinnas hang out. You know those of us who are intelligent enough to know what sin is, and do it anyway." She circled her right hand and continued, "That would be us right here."

Jamie responded, I didn't ask you about how ya' livin' because I already know. Feeling guilty, huh?"

"Bible Girl, please. That's why you came down here. All you do is harass me about Jesus and that Bible you carry around in your backpack, weighing about 10 pounds. That's why you're all bent over," Clarissa mocked.

Jamie fired back, "What's wrong with me talking about Jesus, you know he's 'THE TRUTH'. You know that for yourself, because he healed you from leukemia last year."

"How could I forget? Because he healed me, I've made the decision to live like I wanna live. YOLO-you only live once. I can get saved and go to church when I'm older, and read the Bible too, Bible girl." Clarissa came back.

"Who said you're going to get old, cancer can come back. Who's to say yours won't?" Jamie questioned.

Clarissa was hot, "You know you didn't have to go there. I am doing just fine, so if I wanna do what I wanna do that's what I'll do—smokin, sippin, twerkin, that's what I do, ain't nobody gonna stop me."

Jamie replied, "The sad thing is about you is that you know you're lost and you don't even care. So, I'm out! You know Jesus loves you and is waiting for you to come home, with your lost self."

Clarissa yelled, "Girl bye, and don't come around here no more. Sellout!"

Clarissa jumped down from the hood of Tyrone's car, walked toward the community center thinking, "So what if I'm lost. Jesus knows where to find me. Maybe he ain't looking hard enough. While he's taking his time to find me, I have more time to get it together."

Think about the song, the bible story and the case study.

- Can you relate to or identify with any of the characters? Explain.
- What issues are you wrestling with in the case study, bible story and song?
- How would you describe Clarissa's attitude regarding life and God? Explain.
- What is your attitude towards life and God? Explain.
- If we were to compare Clarissa to the younger son and Jamie to the older son, how do their attitudes and actions mirror the older and younger son in Luke 15?
- How are the song, case study and story connected?

12. Have participants return to their reading partner. Ask them to create a conversation between Clarissa and Jamie after Clarissa receives the news that her Leukemia has returned.
13. Give partners the opportunity to share their conversations with the group.
14. Have partners link up with another partnership to share responses to the following questions about their conversation?
    - What was the theme of your conversation? (sadness, confusion, anger, etc.)
    - How was God present or absent in your conversation? Explain.

15. Have participants return to the large group. Ask, how can we be sure that God is with us wherever we go, or whatever we experience?
16. After students respond, read Psalm 139: 7- 10. Ask, what are these verses saying to you?

**EXPLORING**
**(You'll need the Saved, Now Saved for Real Handout, p .156-159)**

1. Continue by saying, we are going to dig a little deeper and explore the meaning of what it means for God to always be with us. One way of understanding is by exploring the word "grace." Grace can be described in three ways.
    - **Prevenient Grace**—God's love and favor that actively pursues us so we can have a relationship with God.
    - **Justifying Grace**—Grace that convicts us of sin and moves us toward a relationship with God through Jesus Christ.
    - **Sanctifying Grace**—Grace that moves us toward Jesus Christ and helps us to become more like him.
2. Pass out copies of Saved, Now Saved for Real.
3. Ask students to identify and underline examples of prevenient, justifying and sanctifying grace.
4. Read the poem with feeling and conviction.

**Saved, Now Saved for Real**
I wasn't even thinking about giving my life to Christ
Baptized at 8
Church every Sunday I could remember
Baptizing my cats
Serving Holy Communion to my grand folk
THAT WAS MORE THAN ENOUGH
A church girl, "YES"
Saved, "NO"
But then one Sunday, my BFF's heart was touched
I guess
"We're going up front next Sunday to give our lives to Christ and join the church"
"I'm not going up there," I responded
"Yes, we are"
"Whatever"
Singing in the choir, ushering at the door, attending youth group

That's more than enough
Give my life to Christ
Not interested, not today
Definitely not next Sunday
Throughout the week, I never gave it a second thought
The next Sunday, I went to church
Sang a few songs, gave an offering, heard the word
Felt my BFF tugging my hand, "Come on it's time to go up front"
"I'm not going up there"
"Yes, you are"
I gave in, walked down the isle
To the applause of the congregation
Standing there next to my BFF and the pastor
I felt a presence come over me…and…
I started to cry
I could actually feel God's love, his presence
HIS GRACE—as I look back
God had been pursuing me, drawing me
The choir, the ushering, youth group, worship
Were all means of grace
IT WAS A SET UP
Ways in which God demonstrated his active presence in my life
God issued an invitation to abundant, eternal life
I accepted the relationship with him
God's grace came into my life when I needed it most.
On that day, I don't remember the calendar day or month
But during my 14th year of life
I accepted God's gift of grace
From that day to this, God's grace has always been available
It has never disappointed me
At times I've refused it
Even taken advantage of it
Nevertheless, grace was there
Surely, goodness and mercy will follow me all of my days
Not because I've deserved or earned it
But because God is the giver of blessings and favor

SAVED
If you confess with your mouth
SAVED
And believe in your heart
SAVED
That God raised Jesus from the dead
YOU SHALL BE SAVED
Sins forgiven
Relationship with God restored
God's grace alone
Brought me into a right relationship with God
Nothing I did, or could do
God loved me for who I was
Broken, hurt, bitter, consumed with sadness, rebellious, angry…
Wearing the mask
Pretending everything was OK
But not!
I responded in faith to God's gracious invitation of relationship with Jesus the Christ
I am SAVED
Aligned with God, justifying grace, I am in Christ, a new creation, the old has gone
The new has come, life begins
New context, new situation, new circumstances, new outlook, but only for a season
Consumed by the lust of the eyes, the lust of the flesh and the pride of life
Living life on my terms, yet still going to church
Religion not relationship
Slipping in and out of sin
Still churching, not relating, saved but not for real
Wishy washy
Yet covered under the blood
Blessed by grace
But there came a time, when there was a void
A longing, a desire for more
So, I made a decision…to go to Bible study, memorize the word, live the word
It wasn't so easy, trapped in a dilemma, a quandary
Reading the word, studying the word, memorizing the word, but not living the word
But an encounter with an enemy of my faith who questioned and interrogated my religious convictions

"As-Salaam-Alaikum Sister"
"Good morning"
"Want to buy a Final Call"
"No, I'm a Christian."
Then the interrogation began
"Do you know what King James did? Your Bible by King James is...
Stunned, speechless, I didn't know what to say.
Didn't have the presence of mind to lift up the name of Jesus and say
He died for you, He rose again, He loves you, He gives eternal life
Did not and could not defend or witness for my Savior
Felt like an embarrassment to God
Supposed to be his child, his chosen one, yet couldn't defend his honor
If Christ had banished me from his presence, I would have understood
I did not represent him well. I did not witness about his work
I had committed the ultimate mistake, this was the worst I have ever felt
I drove to church with tears in my eyes
How could I make it up to him?
By being saved for real!
So, I confessed again, believed anew
SAVED FOR REAL
A new way of living—Abundance
A new way of loving—With my whole heart
A new way of serving—Loving others
SAVED FOR REAL
You see God loved me too much to let me stay the same
It is sanctifying grace that helps me to understand salvation as a continual process
Constantly and consistently delivered from evil and trouble
Growing and maturing in my ability to live as Jesus lived
Working on my inner thoughts and motives
Working on my outer actions and behaviors
Praying that they align with God's purpose and will
Testifying to my union with God
Yes, I am
SAVED FOR REAL
SERIOUSLY SAVED
In it authentically

And for life eternally
~Richelle B. White

5. Review the definitions of prevenient, justifying and sanctifying grace. Ask participants to share their examples of prevenient, justifying and sanctifying grace from the poem. Allow participants to reread the poem if needed.
6. After participants share their responses, ask the following questions:
   - Do you share any of the same experiences as the writer? Please share.
   - What do you learn about friendship in this poem? What kinds of friends make the best friends?
   - How have you seen prevenient grace active in your life?
   - How does Christ save us?
   - What do you think the author means by "saved for real"? Why is being "saved for real" important?
   - How are the song, case study, Bible story and poem connected? What do you learn about grace from each of them?
7. Close the session with the following call and response:

   Leader: Prevenient, justifying, sanctifying grace. Another way of understanding God's great love for us.

   Group: God's grace is sufficient. His strength is made perfect in my weakness

   All Together: When nothing else would help, grace & mercy was there!

8. Extinguish the candle.

## SESSION THREE—ALL ABOUT THAT GRACE

### SET-UP:

**(You'll need an Afrocentric cloth, large jar candle, candle lighter)**

1. On a table, place a piece of Afrocentric cloth and a large jar candle.
2. Begin by saying: "We light this candle as a symbol of God's grace in our lives."
3. Light the candle; continue the session with "EMERGING."

### EMERGING

**(You'll need the Looking At Our Relationship Handout, p .160)**
**(the font is smaller in this sentence)**

1. Pass out Looking At Our Relationship Handout. Read the directions with the participants.
2. Give participants 12-15 minutes to complete the handout. Allow for additional time if needed.
3. If desired, play soft instrumental music while the participants are working.

**Looking At Our Relationship with the Father**

Being a prodigal or lost child is not just a one-time event, we are often lost, walking away from God, our loving Father by our self-righteous attitudes, acts of disobedience and poor choices. How do you know if you are lost? You might be lost if you wander too far away from God and God's word. You might be lost if you engage in activities that take you away from or take the place of God. Look at the list below. Circle the things that are currently keeping you away from God or has the potential of keeping you away from spending time with God.

| | | | |
|---|---|---|---|
| Friends | Family | iPod/MP3 Player | YouTube |
| Video Games | Facebook | Instagram | Twitter |
| Snapchat | School/Work | Sexual Relationships | Sports |
| Music | Texting | Talking | Television |
| Food | Shopping | Technology | Other |

Identify why each activity takes up so much of your time. What are the possible consequences of spending more time with these activities than with God?

Take a look at the prayer of the younger son in verses 18-19—"I will go to my father and say "Father, I have sinned against both heaven and you, and I am no longer worthy of being called your son. Please take me on as a hired servant." This is a prayer of confession that is seeking forgiveness. Write your own prayer of confession. Telling God of the poor decisions and choices you have made. Then ask God to forgive you.

Wisdom teaches us that once we learn better, we should be compelled to do better. Write an action plan to walk forward and not continue making bad decisions in the future? Outline your plan. For example, I am going to listen to my iPod for only two hours a day, instead of four hours.

4. After the work is complete, say the following prayer:

**Prayer of Confession**

Lord we confess that we have taken advantage of your love and grace. Forgive us and give us a new start. In Jesus name, Amen.

**HONORING**

**(You'll Need the Lost Child Demonstration (see attached Leader Notes—Lost Child Demonstration, p .161)**

1. Ask participants to gather around the table. The materials for the demonstration should already be set up.
2. Share the demonstration with the participants.
3. Share these lessons following the demonstration.
    - All of us lose our way from time to time, and wander away from home.
    - God loves us enough to let us come back home.
    - God's love cleans us up, makes us new, and welcomes us home.
    - Temptations, old habits, unhealthy people will try to come back into our lives.
    - By Keeping it 100 with our loving father, negative influences don't have the power to draw us back to our lost condition.
    - Make it a priority to share with others the word of God and your testimony of God's love.
    - God will love, receive and change them too.
4. Close the session with the following prayer.

**Let us pray**

Father we admit that we are sinners. We've done wrong, we've made poor decisions. We have sinned against others. We've sinned against you. Father, we believe that Jesus is your son. We believe and confess that Jesus is Lord. We believe in our hearts that God raised Jesus from the dead. Thank you God for saving us and welcoming us home. We once were lost, but now we're found. In Jesus name. Amen.

5. Extinguish the candle.

# "All About That Grace" Handouts

# "Looking to Jesus"

**Reader**

"I met a man named Jesus, and I've had an exchange with him. I gave him my sorrows, he gave me his joy; I gave him my confusion, he gave me his peace; I gave him my despair, he gave me his hope; I gave him my hatred, he gave me his love; I gave him my torn life, he gave me his purpose.

(Rev. Otis Moss)

Leader: What did you give Jesus? What did he give you in return?

Group: Ask each person to respond individually to the two questions.

**Let Us Pray (All together)**

Jesus, our savior,
We come.
Jesus, our healer,
We come.
Jesus, our deliverer,
We come.
We come wanting a closer relationship with you.
Lord, prepare our minds to understand your word.
Lord, prepare our hearts to receive your word.
Lord, prepare us to be living examples of your love in our lives.
In Jesus name,
Amen.

## "Lost Hoping To Be Found"

### Case Study—Lost Hoping to Be Found

Clarissa was sitting on the hood of her boo Tyrone's car outside of the community center. Her cousin Jamie walked up to her and said, "What's up girl?"

Clarissa, said "Well, if it ain't Bible Girl, whatcu you doing down here with us heathens? This is where all the sinnas hang out. You know those of us who are intelligent enough to know what sin is, and do it anyway." She circled her right hand and continued, "That would be us right here."

Jamie responded, I didn't ask you about how ya' livin' because I already know. Feeling guilty, huh?"

"Bible Girl, please. That's why you came down here. All you do is harass me about Jesus and that Bible you carry around in your backpack, weighing about 10 pounds. That's why you're all bent over," Clarissa mocked.

Jamie fired back, "What's wrong with me talking about Jesus, you know he's 'THE TRUTH.' You know that for yourself, because he healed you from leukemia last year."

"How could I forget? Because he healed me, I've made the decision to live like I wanna live. YOLO-you only live once. I can get saved and go to church when I'm older, and read the Bible too, Bible girl." Clarissa came back.

"Who said you're going to get old, cancer can come back. Who's to say yours won't?" Jamie questioned.

Clarissa was hot, "You know you didn't have to go there. I am doing just fine, so if I wanna do what I wanna do that's what I'll do—smokin, sippin, twerkin, that's what I do, ain't nobody gonna stop me."

Jamie replied, "The sad thing is about you is that you know you're lost and you don't even care. So, I'm out! You know Jesus loves you and is waiting for you to come home, with your lost self."

Clarissa yelled, "Girl bye, and don't come around here no more. Sellout!"

Clarissa jumped down from the hood of Tyrone's car, walked toward the community center thinking, "So what if I'm lost. Jesus knows where to find me. Maybe he ain't looking hard enough. While he's taking his time to find me, I have more time to get it together."

Think about the song, the bible story and the case study.

- Can you relate to or identify with any of the characters? Explain.
- What issues are you wrestling with in the case study, bible story and song?
- How would you describe Clarissa's attitude regarding life and God? Explain.
- What is your attitude towards life and God? Explain.
- If we were to compare Clarissa to the younger son and Jamie to the older son, how do their attitudes and actions mirror the older and younger son in Luke 15?
- How are the song, case study and story connected?

## "Saved, Now Saved For Real"

Grace can be described in three ways.

- **Prevenient Grace—**God's love and favor that actively pursues us so we can have a relationship with God.
- **Justifying Grace—**Grace that convicts of sin and moves us toward a relationship with God through Jesus Christ.
- **Sanctifying Grace—**Grace that moves us toward Jesus Christ and helps us to become more like him.

Read the poem. Identify and underline examples of prevenient, justifying and sanctifying grace.

**Saved, Now Saved for Real...**
I wasn't even thinking about giving my life to Christ
Baptized at 8
Church every Sunday I could remember
Baptizing my cats
Serving Holy Communion to my grand folk
THAT WAS MORE THAN ENOUGH
A church girl, "YES"
Saved, "NO"
But then one Sunday, my BFF's heart was touched
I guess
"We're going up front next Sunday to give our lives to Christ and join the church"
"I'm not going up there," I responded
"Yes, we are"
"Whatever"
Singing in the choir, ushering at the door, attending youth group
That's more than enough
Give my life to Christ
Not interested, not today
Definitely not next Sunday
Throughout the week, I never gave it a second thought
The next Sunday, I went to church
Sang a few songs, gave an offering, heard the word
Felt my BFF tugging my hand, "Come on it's time to go up front"
"I'm not going up there"

"Yes, you are"
I gave in, walked down the isle
To the applause of the congregation
Standing there next to my BFF and the pastor
I felt a presence come over me…and…
I started to cry
I could actually feel God's love, his presence
HIS GRACE—as I look back
God had been pursuing me, drawing me
The choir, the ushering, youth group, worship
Were all means of grace
IT WAS A SET UP
Ways in which God demonstrated his active presence in my life
God issued an invitation to abundant, eternal life
I accepted the relationship with him
God's grace came into my life when I needed it most.
On that day, I don't remember the calendar day or month
But during my 14th year of life
I accepted God's gift of grace
From that day to this, God's grace has always been available
It has never disappointed me
At times I've refused it
Even taken advantage of it
Nevertheless, grace was there
Surely, goodness and mercy will follow me all of my days
Not because I've deserved or earned it
But because God is the giver of blessings and favor
SAVED
If you confess with your mouth
SAVED
And believe in your heart
SAVED
That God raised Jesus from the dead
YOU SHALL BE SAVED
Sins forgiven
Relationship with God restored

God's grace alone
Brought me into a right relationship with God
Nothing I did, or could do
God loved me for who I was
Broken, hurt, bitter, consumed with sadness, rebellious, angry...
Wearing the mask
Pretending everything was OK
But not!
I responded in faith to God's gracious invitation of relationship with Jesus the Christ
I am SAVED
Aligned with God, justifying grace, I am in Christ, a new creation, the old has gone,
The new has come, life begins
New context, new situation, new circumstances, new outlook, but only for a season
Consumed by the lust of the eyes, the lust of the flesh and the pride of life
Living life on my terms, yet still going to church
Religion not relationship
Slipping in and out of sin
Still churching, not relating, saved but not for real
Wishy washy
Yet covered under the blood
Blessed by grace
But there came a time, when there was a void
A longing, a desire for more
So, I made a decision...to go to Bible study, memorize the word, and live the word
It wasn't so easy, trapped in a dilemma, a quandary
Reading the word, studying the word, memorizing the word, but not living the word
But an encounter with an enemy of my faith who questioned and interrogated my religious convictions
"As-Salaam-Alaikum Sister"
"Good morning"
"Want to buy a Final Call"
"No, I'm a Christian."
Then the interrogation began
"Do you know what King James did? Your Bible by King James is...
Stunned, speechless, I didn't know what to say.
Didn't have the presence of mind to lift up the name of Jesus and say
He died for you, He rose again, He loves you, He gives eternal life

Did not and could not defend or witness for my Savior
Felt like an embarrassment to God
Supposed to be his child, his chosen one, yet couldn't defend his honor
If Christ had banished me from his presence, I would have understood
I did not represent him well. I did not witness about his work
I had committed the ultimate mistake, this was the worst I have ever felt
I drove to church with tears in my eyes
How could I make it up to him?
By being saved for real!
So, I confessed again, believed anew
SAVED FOR REAL
A new way of living—Abundance
A new way of loving—With my whole heart
A new way of serving—Loving others
SAVED FOR REAL
You see God loved me too much to let me stay the same
It is sanctifying grace that helps me to understand salvation as a continual process
Constantly and consistently delivered from evil and trouble
Growing and maturing in my ability to live as Jesus lived
Working on my inner thoughts and motives
Working on my outer actions and behaviors
Praying that they align with God's purpose and will
Testifying to my union with God
Yes, I am
SAVED FOR REAL
SERIOUSLY SAVED
In it authentically
And for life eternally

- Do you share any of the same experiences as the writer? Please share.
- What do you learn about friendship in this poem? What kinds of friends make the best friends?
- How have you seen prevenient grace active in your life?
- How does Christ save us?
- What do you think the author means by "saved for real?" Why is being "saved for real" important?
- How are the song, case study, bible story and poem connected? What do you learn about grace from each of them?

## "Looking At Our Relationship with the Father"

Being a prodigal or lost child is not just a one-time event, we are often lost, walking away from God, our loving Father by our self-righteous attitudes, acts of disobedience and poor choices. How do you know if you are lost? You might be lost if you wander too far away from God and God's word. You might be lost if you engage in activities that take you away from or take the place of God. Look at the list below. Circle the things that are currently keeping you away from God or has the potential of keeping you away from spending time with God.

| | | | |
|---|---|---|---|
| Friends | Family | iPod/MP3 Player | YouTube |
| Video Games | Facebook | Instagram | Twitter |
| Snapchat | School/Work | Sexual Relationships | Sports |
| Music | Texting | Talking | Television |
| Food | Shopping | Technology | Other |

Identify why each activity takes up so much of your time. What are the possible consequences of spending more time with these activities than with God?

Take a look at the prayer of the younger son in verses 18-19—"I will go to my father and say "Father, I have sinned against both heaven and you, and I am no longer worthy of being called your son. Please take me on as a hired servant." This is a prayer of confession that is seeking forgiveness. Write your own prayer of confession. Telling God of the poor decisions and choices you have made. Then ask God to forgive you. (Use the space below and the back if necessary)

Wisdom teaches us that once we learn better, we should be compelled to do better. Write an action plan to walk forward and not continue making bad decisions in the future. Outline your plan. For example, I am going to listen to my iPod for only two hours a day, instead of four hours.

## LEADER NOTES

### "The Lost Child Demonstration"

This demonstration helps students to understand that they can always come home to their Father's (God's) house. Materials needed include:

- Iodine (in a bottle labeled poor choices, decisions, sinful behaviors that move us away from God)
- Water (represents growing relationship and fellowship with God through His word and fellowship)
- Water/Iodine mix (in a labeled bottle marked negative influences, unhealthy people)
- Oxiclean (in a container labeled the Father's love)
- Two-16 ounce clear plastic glasses

1. Pour water into one of the glasses, telling students what the water represents.
2. Pour the iodine into the glass with the water. Tell students what the iodine represents.
3. Ask students to describe what happened to the water, reminding them what the water represents.
4. Say, it seems like we're lost, but we can always come home to the Father.
5. Pour some oxiclean in the glass (telling them what the oxiclean represents).
6. Twirl the mixture containing oxiclean, iodine & water. As the oxiclean mixes with the iodine and water, it will take the stain of the iodine out.
7. Say to the students, the Father's love has welcomed you home and made you clean again.
8. Take out the bottle with the water/iodine mix. Tell the students what it represents.
9. Pour the iodine/mixture into the cleaned solution. The stained solution will be immediately cleaned.
10. Say negative influences, unhealthy people can tempt you but they can't draw you away from God, the Father.
11. Pour some of the water/iodine mix in the clean glass (reminding students what it is)
12. Pour some of the clean water solution into the stained mixture glass.
13. The stained solution will also turn clean.
14. Telling others about the Father's love, and his word will change others.

The Lessons

1. All of us lose our way from time to time, and wander away from home.
2. God loves us enough to let us come back home.
3. God's love and God's word cleans us up, makes us new, welcomes us home.
4. Temptations, old habits, unhealthy people will try to come back into our lives.
5. By Keeping it 100 with our loving Father, negative influences don't have the power to draw us back to our lost condition.
6. Make it a priority to share with others the word of God and your testimony of God's love.
7. God will love, receive and change them too.

# Appendix D

# "Goodbye Fear, Hello Courage"

**Discipleship Goal: Character Development**

Character development is an intentional lifelong process of growth and progress. The goal of character development involves defining one's fundamental values, prioritizing and living out one's moral principles on a daily basis.

**Time Needed**: 3 sessions of 60-75 minutes

**Song**: "Glory"—John Legend featuring Common

**Session Objectives:**

1. Participants will explore the message in the music and identify characteristics that lead to courageous actions.
2. Participants will examine the role of fear and discuss ways to approach fear that would embody courageous actions.
3. Participants will create their own artistic compositions about courage.

**Main Idea:**

When we exhibit courage, bravery, boldness, confidence, resolve, we are displaying who we really are and what we are made of. However, our arch enemy "fear" likes to take up residence in our lives; that enemy seeks to hinder us from being who we truly are and accomplishing all that God has purposed for us to do. What is our response? Goodbye fear, hello courage.

**Directions to the Session Leaders:**

Prior to teaching this lesson, please complete the following:

- Pray for direction, creativity and conviction.
- Read the entire lesson plan including the leader notes—Thinking About Fears, Affirmations, Prayer Stones.
- Read the Bible passages identified.
- Listen to "Glory."
- Watch the YouTube video, "John Legend—Glory Feat Common Lyrics." (4:26)
- Watch scenes 6 (32:36-36:29) and 9 (1:10:33- 1:20:22) from the DVD *"Selma."*
- Print song lyrics for each participant. Lyrics can be found at www.azlyrics.com or www.song-lyrics.com.
- Print lesson handouts for each participant. Handouts are located at the end of the lesson in order of use.
- Gather all session materials.
- Be open to the moving of the Holy Spirit during discussions, conversations and activities.

## SESSION ONE—GOODBYE FEAR, HELLO COURAGE

### SET-UP

**(You'll need an Afrocentric cloth, large jar candle, candle lighter)**

1. On a table place a piece of Afrocentric cloth and a large jar candle.
2. Begin by saying, "We light this candle to celebrate the courage of our African American Ancestors and our growing courage within."
3. Light the candle. Continue the session with "INVITING."

### INVITING

**(You'll need Living to Show God's Grace Handout, p .178)**

1. Divide participants into five small groups if possible. Label each group with one of these terms: Dream, Justice, Faith, Grace, Strength.
2. Each small group should stand in a circle.
3. Read, "Living to Show God's Grace, "Invite each group to read the phrases that correspond with the group's name

**Living to Show God's Grace**

**Dream:**

Inside my head there lives a dream. I want to build a better world.

**Justice**:

Where justice, love and peace rule. But I fear criticism and ridicule.

**Faith:**

So, I put off my dream for tomorrow. It's time to step on faith

**Grace:**

Gotta show God's grace. Fear no longer has me bound.

**Courage:**

Look what I have found. I've got strength, courage and resilience.

**Everyone:**

It's been inside of me all along.

(words adapted from "Strength, Courage & Wisdom" by India.Arie)

4. Have participants return to their seats.

**LISTENING**

**(You'll need the CD/MP3 file—"Glory" by John Legend featuring Common , or YouTube video, "John Legend—Glory Feat Common Lyrics" (4:26), and lyrics to "Glory" for each participant)**

1. Introduce the song "Glory" by saying, "Glory is a song performed by rapper Common and recording artist John Legend. It is the theme song from the 2014 film *"Selma"* which teaches about the 1965 Selma to Montgomery marches. Selma and Montgomery are cities in Alabama. As you listen, pay attention to the words, thoughts or actions that display courage."
2. Pass out lyrics to each participant.
3. Play the song.
4. After listening ask the following questions:
    - What is the message of the song?
    - What history lessons/personalities does the song mention?
    - What did you hear that speaks about courage?
    - Why is the word "glory" important to this song? What does it stand for?
    - What "war" might the artists be talking about? (justice, freedom, equality)
    - How can younger and older people work together to achieve their goals?
    - How do you define courage? (Courage means doing the right thing even when it's scary or difficult. It means that you try your best to succeed, even when success isn't guaranteed)

**CONNECTING**

**(You'll need pens, pencils, Courage Mosaic Handout, p .179)**

1. Open this section by saying, "Dr. Martin Luther King, Jr. said 'The time is always right to do what's right.' Share some instances when it becomes difficult to do the right thing."
2. After providing some time for conversation, transition with these words: "Courage means doing the right thing even when it's scary or difficult. Today we are going to examine the lives of people who lived during the 1965 marches—from Selma, Alabama to Montgomery, Alabama."
3. Distribute the Courage Mosaic handout to participants.
4. Read the directions. Divide participants into pairs. Give them a few minutes to record their responses and assist each other in completing their individual mosaics.

**Courage Mosaic—Complete as many of the boxes as you can.**

| | | |
|---|---|---|
| A story, movie, TV show, book about courage: | Fictional characters who display courage: | Real people who display courage: |
| Synonyms for Courage: | Define Courage: | Antonyms for courage: |
| A time that I had courage was... | One more thing about courage: | A time when I wish I had more courage... |

5. Engage the whole group in discussion using the following questions:
   - In what ways do people demonstrate courage in the stories, movies, TV shows, books you have seen or read?
   - In what ways do people you know demonstrate courage?
   - In what ways are these demonstrations of courage similar or different?
   - How have you demonstrated courage in the past?
   - Is courage demonstrated in large heroic efforts? Explain.
   - Is courage demonstrated in small ways? Please share.
   - What Bible stories have you heard about courage? (Joseph, Joshua, Noah, Moses, Jesus, Esther, Daniel)
   - What stories from Black History have you heard/read about that demonstrate courage?
   - What difference do these (Bible and Black History) make in our lives?
   - What is one more thing you would share about courage?
6. End the session with the following quote by Rosa Parks, "You must never be fearful when what you are doing when it is right."
7. Ask students to repeat the following declaration, "Goodbye Fear, Hello Courage."
8. Extinguish the candle.

## SESSION TWO—GOODBYE FEAR, HELLO COURAGE

### SET-UP

**(You'll need an Afrocentric cloth, large jar candle, candle lighter)**

1. On a table place a piece of Afrocentric cloth and a large jar candle.
2. Begin by saying, "We light this candle to celebrate the courage of our African American ancestors and our growing courage within."
3. Light the candle. Continue the session with "ENGAGING."

### ENGAGING

**(You'll need Bibles, pens, pencils, slips of paper, container to collect slips of paper)**

1. Have students open their Bibles to 1 Samuel 17.
2. Allow students to take turns reading, the following verses: (1-7, 8-11, 12-16, 17-24)

After reading, ask the following questions:

- Who is opposing each other? (v. 1-3)
- Describe the giant (v. 4-7) Why were the men of Israel so afraid of the giant?
- How did Saul and his troops feel after hearing the challenges of Goliath? (v. 11)
- Do you ever feel like the Israelites when confronting giants/fears in your own life? Please share.
- Who is David? (v. 12-15)
- What did David discover when he went to camp to check on his brothers?

3. Continue reading verses: (25-28. 29-33. 34-37. 38-44). After reading, ask the following questions:
    - Why did David consider fighting the Philistine giant? (v. 24-25)
    - Describe David's attitude toward Goliath? (v. 26)
    - How did David encourage Saul? (v. 32)
    - What was King Saul's response? (v. 33)
    - How did King Saul discourage David from fighting?
    - Have you ever wanted to stand against your giants/fears and became discouraged? Share your experience. In the midst of your discouragement, what did you do?
    - Why was David so confident in his ability to beat Goliath? (v.34-37)
    - What did Saul say to David? (v. 37)
    - David tried to fight in King Saul's armor, why didn't he? (v. 38-39)
    - What weapons did David choose to use? (v. 40)
    - What does David teach us about confronting giants/fears?

4. Continue reading verses: (45-47, 48-53, 54-58). After reading, ask the following questions:
    - Who was with David as he fought the giant? (v. 45-47)
    - What words does David use to describe God and what God will do? (v. 45-47)
    - How did David beat the Philistine? (v. 50)
    - Describe what the men of Israel did after David defeated the Philistine giant. (v. 52-54)
    - Who will be with you when you face your giants? How has God been there for you in other times? Share your testimony.
    - What is one lesson that you can take from David's story to apply to your own life?
5. Introduce the "Thinking About Fears" activity.

**Leader Notes—Thinking About Fears**

The Thinking About Fears discussion activity provides participants the opportunity to talk about fears they may have and think of healthy ways to approach the fears by identifying acts of courage to overcome them.

- Distribute 2-3 slips of paper to each participant.
- Ask participants to write down 2-3 fears, one on each slip of paper. Write anonymously, do not sign your name.
- Pass around a container to collect the fears.
- Take turns choosing and reading aloud one fear at a time.
- Collectively discuss ways to approach the fears that exemplifies courage to overcome them.

**Example**

Fear—Being cyberbullied

Overcoming—tell my parents, print messages received, delete comments, share messages with the principal.

Other Examples of fears that teens may be experiencing include

- Loss of friends
- Test taking
- Talking to parents about personal problems
- Home life
- School life
- Peer pressure—not fitting in
- Depression
- Suicide
- Not getting good grades
- Life after graduation

6. After a time of sharing, ask the following questions:
   - Courage has boundaries. When might you be risking too much when facing a fear? (In the cyberbullying example, risking too much might be drawing the line in reporting the incident by not wanting to ruin the reputation of the bully to make yourself look good)
   - How can we help each other with our fears? (accountability, support, encouragement)
   - What other resources do we have to help us with our fears?
   - What have you experienced today that might help you as you face and overcome your fears?

**EXPLORING**

**(You'll need pens, pencils, journals, *Selma* DVD—scene 6 (32:36-36:29) and scene 9 (1:10:331:20:22, Selma to Montgomery Courage Under Fire Handout, p .180-181)**

1. Pass out the Selma to Montgomery—Courage Under Fire Handout to all participants.
2. Continue by asking, "Why is Selma important in Black history, in American history?" (voting rights)
3. Choose a volunteer to read the first paragraph, "Background," from the handout.

**Selma to Montgomery—Courage Under Fire**

**Background**—In 1965, there were three Selma to Montgomery marches that were a part of the Voting Rights Movement taking place in Selma, Alabama. Although segregation had ended, Blacks were still being denied the right to vote. African American protesters decided to walk 54 miles from Selma to the Alabama state capital of Montgomery, showing their desire to vote. This showed courage under fire. There were several African American men and women leaders at this time who showed bravery and a sense of determination to do what was right. They are Jimmie Lee Jackson, Annie Lee Cooper, John Lewis and James Bevel.

4. After reading, show scene 6 from the *Selma* DVD (32:36–36:29)
5. Choose volunteers to read paragraphs 2, 3, 4, 5 under "Profiles in Courage" on the handout.

**Profiles in Courage**

**Jimmie Lee Jackson**—Jimmie Lee Jackson was a young man who became a part of the Civil Rights Movement. He was an activist and a deacon in his church. His desire was for his 84-year-old grandfather to be able to vote. Jimmie Lee was marching peacefully on February 26, 1965. He was shot to death by a state trooper in Marion, Alabama. Jackson's death inspired a voting rights march.

**Annie Lee Cooper**—Annie Lee Cooper also wanted to exercise her right to vote. On one particular day, she stood for hours in line outside of the county courthouse to register to vote. The sheriff insisted that she go home; he poked her in the back of the neck with a 'billy club.' Annie Lee turned and punched

Sheriff Clark in the jaw. She was wrestled to the ground, arrested, charged with assault and attempted murder. She stayed in jail for 11 hours.

**John Lewis**—John Lewis was the youngest of the Civil Rights leaders during that time. He was the president of the Student Nonviolent Coordinating Committee (SNCC). As president of SNCC, he opened Freedom Schools, launched Mississippi Freedom Summer, organized voter registration and was one of the 13 original Freedom Riders. He had been arrested 24 times in the nonviolent struggle for equal justice. Lewis was a prominent leader in the Selma to Montgomery marches. He, along with others, led over 600 marchers across the Edmund Pettus Bridge in Selma, Alabama.

**James Bevel**—James Bevel was the director of Selma's voting rights movement. He called for a march from Selma to Montgomery. This march led the United States Congress to pass the 1965 Voting Rights Act.

6. After reading, ask the following questions:
   - Which Profile in Courage caught your attention? Why?
   - Do courageous people set out to make history, or is it about doing the right thing? What are your thoughts?
7. Choose one volunteer to read the paragraph, "Three Marches," on the handout.

**Selma to Montgomery**

**Three Marches**—600 marchers gathered in Selma on Sunday, March 7 and crossed the Edmund Pettus Bridge over the Alabama River on their way to Montgomery. Their way was blocked by Alabama State Troopers and local police who ordered them to turn around. The marching protesters refused. The officers shot tear gas, and went into the crowd beating the non-violent protesters with billy clubs. Over 50 people were hospitalized. This day called Bloody Sunday was televised around the world. On March 9, Martin Luther King, Jr. led a second march, but turned around at the same bridge. On March 21, the marchers were protected by federal officials and they made it to Montgomery. On August 1965, the federal Voting Rights Act was passed which was aimed to overcome legal barriers at the state and local levels that prevented African Americans from exercising the right to vote under the 15$^{th}$ amendment to the United States Constitution.[187]

8. After reading, show Scene 9 from the *"Selma"* DVD (1:10:33 – 1:20:22).
9. After viewing, scene 9, ask the following questions:
   - What does courage look like in this scene? (marchers were not afraid, marched for a cause, did the right thing)
   - What do you learn about courage from these nonviolent protesters?

- How were these protesters different from the protesters we see today?
- What are your views of protesting? What would you protest for? What would be your strategy?

10. Read "Acts of Courage—Summary" from the handout.

**Acts of Courage**

**Summary**—The courageous men and women faced threats, beatings, lynching, harassment and other forms of abuse simply because they wanted access to their constitutional right to vote. Their courage was heroic. Their sacrifice, determination and effort are to be honored. They did great things for our generation and the generations to come. Their actions have made history. Every act of courage is great, whether large or small. It takes determination and bravery to overcome fear and frustration.

Think about a fear that you will need courage to conquer. It may be trying out for an athletic/cheerleading team, standing up to a bully, applying to college or asking someone you like on a date. Where are you being called to be courageous?

11. After giving participants a few minutes to respond to the concluding question, encourage students to stand and repeat the following quote by Dr. Martin Luther King, Jr. "The time is always right to do what is right."
12. Extinguish the candle.

## SESSION THREE—GOODBYE FEAR, HELLO COURAGE

### SET-UP

**(You'll need Afrocentric cloth, large jar candle, candle lighter)**

1. On a table place a piece of Afrocentric cloth and a large jar candle.
2. Begin by saying, "We light this candle to celebrate the courage of our African American ancestors and our growing courage within."
3. Light the candle. Continue the session with "EMERGING."

### EMERGING

**((You'll need journals, pens, pencils, lightly colored smooth stones (can be purchased at craft, home improvement stores—5 stones per participant, Black sharpie/permanent markers, index cards, and Five Smooth Stones Handout, p .182-183)**

1. Encourage students to open their bibles to Joshua 1:9, read together.
2. Have students join in pairs. Encourage them to read Joshua 1:9 aloud to each other.
3. Give each participant an index card.
4. Introduce "Affirmations."

**Leader Notes—Affirmations**

An affirmation is a positive statement that you can tell yourself often throughout the day. The affirmation might be about something you want to accomplish (ex. I will be successful and work hard in reaching my goals). The affirmation might be about how you feel (ex. Today I feel like a million dollars). The affirmation might be about something you want to become or be (ex. I am a boldly, believing, beautiful creation of God).

5. Encourage participants to read Joshua 1:9 again, individually.
6. Have them write an affirmation that comes from the verse (ex. I am strong and courageous. I won't be afraid or discouraged. God is with me everywhere I go).
7. After participants complete their affirmations, gather in an "Affirmation Circle."
8. Give participants the opportunity to share their affirmation, reading/reciting with confidence and conviction.
9. After sharing, have students return to seats. Briefly review, the story of David and Goliath. Highlight that Joshua overcame his fears because God was with him.
10. Ask participants:
    - How are Joshua and David alike?
    - How did Joshua conquer his fears?
    - What did David use to defeat Goliath?

11. Give each participant 5 lightly colored smooth stones and a sharpie/permanent marker.
12. Explain, These five stones are symbols of the positive character traits or habits that will be helpful when you face your giants/fears. Think about one of those giants/fears that you are facing right now. What character traits to you need to overcome them? You have five stones; write one trait on each stone.
13. Pass out "Five Smooth Stones" Handout. Read the directions.

**Five Smooth Stones**

David used a sling and five smooth stones to defeat the giant Goliath. However, he did not fight the battle alone, God was with him. He trusted in God to give him what he needed to win the victory. You have been given "five smooth stones." These stones are a symbol of the positive character traits or habits that will be helpful when you face your giants and fears. God gives us these tools to overcome.

**Positive Character Traits**

Choose five words from the word bank below to decorate each of your stones. Circle the words that speak to you; words that will help you overcome your giants. Write that word on one of your stones. You may also choose positive character traits that are not listed in the word bank.

Place your stones in a place where you can see them on a regular basis. God has given these traits as tools like he gave the rocks to David. This will be a reminder that God has equipped you to overcome those things that desire to hold you back and keep you in fear.

**Word Bank**

abstinence, acceptance, accountability, ambition, assertiveness, attentiveness, authenticity, awareness, boldness, bravery, calmness, caring, cheerfulness, commitment, compassion, concern, confidence, cooperation, courage, creativity, dependability, determination, dignity, discernment, discipline, empathy, endurance, energy, enthusiasm, excellence, faith, fearlessness, flexibility, focus, forgiveness, fortitude, generosity, grace, gratitude, happiness, harmony, helpfulness, honesty, hope, humility, imagination, independence, innovation, integrity, joyfulness, justice, kindness, knowledge, leadership, love, loyalty, modesty, motivation, obedience, optimism, peace, perseverance, persistence, persuasiveness, politeness, positivity, respect, responsibility, self-control, self-discipline, selflessness, self-respect, sensitivity, seriousness, service, sharing, strength, thankfulness, trust, truthfulness, understanding, uniqueness, unity, vision, wisdom.

14. After participants have designed their stones, have them gather in pairs.

**HONORING**

**(You'll need each person's five smooth stones, Bibles, journals, pens, and pencils)**

1. In pairs, encourage participants to pray using their five smooth stones to confront their fears and face their giants.

**Leader Notes—Prayer Stones**

Participants will help each other write prayers using the words written on their five smooth stones. Ask students to write a prayer using each word they have chosen. See the example below based on the traits of authenticity, integrity, kindness, love and faith.

**Sample Prayer:**

Dear Lord, I sometimes fear that I act fake just to have friends. Please help me to be authentic and true to myself. Lord, sometimes telling the truth and being honest scares me, because people may not like me when I speak my mind. Help me to walk in integrity. Lord, help me to be kind and love others. Lord, I don't always trust you like I should, please increase my faith. In Jesus' name. Amen.

2. Give students the opportunities to share their prayers with the group.
3. Before ending the session, ask students to repeat, "Goodbye fear—Hello courage."
4, Extinguish the candle.

# "Goodbye Fear, Hello Courage" Handouts

## Living to Show God's Grace

**Dream:**
Inside my head there lives a dream. I want to build a better world.

**Justice**:
Where justice, love and peace rule. But I fear criticism and ridicule.

**Faith:**
So, I put off my dream for tomorrow. It's time to step on faith

**Grace:**
Gotta show God's grace. Fear no longer has me bound.

**Courage:**
Look what I have found. I've got strength, courage and resilience.

**Everyone:**
It's been inside of me all along.

(words adapted from Strength, Courage & Wisdom by India.Arie)

**Courage Mosaic—Complete as many of the boxes as you can.**

| A story, movie, TV show, book about courage: | Fictional characters who display courage: | Real people who display courage: |
|---|---|---|
| Synonyms for Courage: | Define Courage: | Antonyms for courage: |
| A time that I had courage was… | One more thing about courage: | A time when I wish I had more courage... |

## *Selma to Montgomery—Courage Under Fire*

**Background**—In 1965, there were three Selma to Montgomery marches that were a part of the Voting Rights Movement taking place in Selma, Alabama. Although segregation had ended, Blacks were still being denied the right to vote. African American protesters decided to walk 54 miles from Selma to the Alabama state capital of Montgomery, showing their desire to vote. This showed courage under fire. There were several African American men and women were leaders at this time who showed bravery and a sense determination to do what was right. They are Jimmie Lee Jackson, Annie Lee Cooper, John Lewis and James Bevel.

**Profiles in Courage**

- **Jimmie Lee Jackson**—Jimmie Lee Jackson was a young man who became a part of the Civil Rights Movement. He was an activist and a deacon in his church. His desire was for his 84-year-old grandfather to be able to vote. Jimmie Lee was marching peacefully on February 26, 1965. He was shot to death by a state trooper in Marion, Alabama. Jackson's death inspired a voting rights march.
- **Annie Lee Cooper**—Annie Lee Cooper also wanted to exercise her right to vote. On one particular day, she stood for hours in line outside of the county courthouse to register to vote. The sheriff insisted that she go home; he poked her in the back of the neck with a 'billy club.' Annie Lee turned and punched Sheriff Clark in the jaw. She was wrestled to the ground, arrested, charged with assault and attempted murder. She stayed in jail for 11 hours.
- **John Lewis—**John Lewis was the youngest of the Civil Rights leaders during that time. He was the president of the Student Nonviolent Coordinating Committee (SNCC). As president of SNCC, he opened Freedom Schools, launched Mississippi Freedom Summer, organized voter registration and was one of the 13 original Freedom Riders. He had been arrested 24 times in the nonviolent struggle for equal justice. Lewis was a prominent leader in the Selma to Montgomery marches. He along with others, led over 600 marchers across the Edmund Pettus Bridge in Selma, Alabama.
- **James Bevel—**James Bevel was the director of Selma's voting rights movement. He called for a march from Selma to Montgomery. This march led the United States Congress to pass the 1965 Voting Rights Act.

**Selma to Montgomery: Three Marches**—600 marchers gathered in Selma on Sunday, March 7, crossed the Edmund Pettus Bridge over the Alabama River on their way to Montgomery. Their way was blocked by Alabama State Troopers and local police who ordered them to turn around. The marching protesters refused. The officers shot tear gas and went into the crowd beating the non-violent protesters with billy clubs. Over 50 people were hospitalized. This day called Bloody Sunday was televised around the world. On March 9, Martin Luther King, Jr led a second march, but turned around at the same bridge. On March

21, the marchers were protected by federal officials and they made it to Montgomery. On August 1965, the federal Voting Rights Act was passed which was aimed to overcome legal barriers at the state and local levels that prevented African Americans from exercising the right to vote under the $15^{th}$ amendment to the United States Constitution.

**Acts of Courage**—The courageous men and women faced threats, beatings, lynching, harassment and other forms of abuse simply because they wanted access to their constitutional right to vote. Their courage was heroic. Their sacrifice, determination and effort are to be honored. They did great things for our generation and the generations to come. Their actions have made history. Every act of courage is great, whether large or small. It takes determination and bravery to overcome fear and frustration. Think about a fear that you will need an act of courage to conquer. It may be trying out for an athletic/cheerleading team, standing up to a bully, applying to college or asking someone you like on a date. Where are you being called to be courageous?

## Five Smooth Stones

David used a sling and five smooth stones to defeat the giant Goliath. However, he did not fight the battle alone, God was with him. He trusted in God to give him what he needed to win the victory. You have been given "five smooth stones." These stones are a symbol of the positive character traits of habits that will be helpful when you face your giants and fears. These are tools that God gives us to overcome.

### Positive Character Traits

Choose five words from the word bank below to decorate each of your stones. Circle the words that speak to you; these traits will help you overcome your giants. Write that word on one of your stones. You may also choose positive character traits that are not listed in the word bank.

Place your stones in a place where you can see them on a regular basis. God has given these traits as tools like he gave the rocks to David. This will be a reminder that God has equipped you to overcome those things that desire to hold you back and keep you in fear.

### Word Bank

abstinence
acceptance
ambition
assertiveness,
attentiveness
authenticity
awareness
boldness
bravery
caring
cheerfulness
commitment
compassion
concern
confidence
courage
creativity,
dependability
determination
discernment
discipline
wisdom
empath
endurance
enthusiasm
excellence
faith
fearlessnes
focus
forgiveness
fortitude
generosity
grace
gratitude
happiness
harmony
helpfulness
hope
humility
imagination
independence
innovation
integrity
joyfulness
justice
kindness
leadership
love
obedience
optimism
peace
perseverance
persistence
persuasiveness
politeness
positivity
respect
responsibility
self-control
self-discipline

selflessness
self-respect
sensitivity
service,
sharing
strength
thankfulness
trust
truthfulness
understanding
uniqueness unity

# Appendix E

# "A Hair Journey"

**Discipleship Goal: Historical-Cultural Enlightenment**

Historical-Cultural Enlightenment is engaging and motivating youth in the retelling the stories of African diasporic people; leading to a historically enlightened constituency of Black youth that understand the Black historical and cultural experience.

**Time Needed:** 3 sessions of 60-75 minutes

**Song:** "I am Not My Hair"—India.Arie

**Session Objectives:**

1. Participants will engage the message in the music and will classify various African American hairstyles as being good or bad hair.
2. Participants will critically engage the biblical texts to decipher inward and outward standards of beauty. They will explore historical and contemporary meanings of good and bad hair.
3. Participants will compose a creative writing piece entitled, "Homage to Black Hair," and celebrate themselves as God's image bearers.

**Main Idea:**

Good hair. Bad hair. Style. Color. Texture. Long. Straight. Short. Nappy. For decades, Black hair has been a topic of interest and a billion dollar business. In addition to being popular, it has also sparked controversy. Whatever your stance or position on black hair, "It's all good," because God says so—Genesis 1:31.

**Directions to the Session Leaders:**

Prior to teaching this lesson, please complete the following:

- Pray for direction, creativity and conviction.
- Read the entire lesson plan, including leader notes—Good and Bad Hair, Hair Story Timeline, Paying Homage
- Read the Bible passages as identified.
- Listen to "I am Not My Hair."
- Watch the YouTube video, "India.Arie—I am not my hair" (with Lyrics) (3:43)
- Print song lyrics for each participant. Lyrics can be found at www.azlyrics.com or www.song-lyrics.com.
- Watch the YouTube Video, "School daze. good and bad hair" (6:08) or scene 7—"Straight and Nappy" from the DVD *School Daze* by Spike Lee
- Watch scenes 2 and 3 (Sit Back and Relax, Burn of the Perm) [11:00-25:00] from the DVD *Good Hair* by Chris Rock
- Print lesson handouts for each participant. Handouts are located at the end of the lesson plan in order of use.
- Gather all session materials.
- Be open to the moving of the Holy Spirit during discussions, conversations and activities.

## SESSION ONE—A HAIR JOURNEY

### SET-UP

**(You'll need an Afrocentric cloth, large jar candle, candle lighter)**

1. On a table place a piece of Africentric cloth and a large jar candle.
2. Begin by saying, "We light this candle and ask God's presence to be with us as we study and take a hair journey that will inform, enlighten and encourage us to love the hair that God has blessed us with. In Jesus name, Amen".
3. Light the candle. Continue the session with "INVITING."

### INVITING

**(You'll need index cards, pens, and pencils)**

1. Start this segment by saying, "Today we will be taking a hair journey, having a critical discussion about black hair and explore historical and contemporary meanings of good and bad hair."
2. Distribute an index card, pencil or pen to each participant.
3. Give the following directions. "Write one statement about your hair on one side of the card."
4. After everyone has written their statement, gather in a circle.
5. Each person should share their hair statement.
6. After each participant reads their statement the group should respond: "We are not our hair."
7. Tell participants to keep their cards to use later in the lesson.

### LISTENING

**(You'll need the CD/MP3 file—"I am Not My Hair" by India.Arie or the YouTube video, "India. Arie—I am not my hair (with Lyrics)" (3:43), and lyrics to "I am Not My Hair" by India.Arie)**

1. Pass out lyrics to each participant.
2. Play the song.
3. After listening ask the following questions:
   - What is India's message to her listeners?
   - What stands out to you from the song?
   - What made India come to the realization that "she is not her hair"?
   - How does India define "good hair" and "bad hair"?
   - Is hair important to you? Why? Why not? Explain.

## CONNECTING

**(You'll need pictures/images of various African American hairstyles, copy paper—8 .5"x11", markers, pens, pencils, Good Hair, Bad Hair handout, p .196)**

### Leader Notes—Good and Bad Hair

Log onto Google Images to search for pictures/images of at least ten of the persons listed below. You will observe a variety of hairstyles. Choose various hairstyles to serve as representatives of good and bad hair. Print the pictures for use in the good and bad hair activity. Number each photo.

| | | | |
|---|---|---|---|
| Michelle Obama | Lil' Wayne | D. L. Hughley | Ledisi |
| Bob Marley | Jurnee Smollett-Bell | Jamie Foxx | Bryshere Y. Gray |
| Latice Crawford | Gabby Douglass | Gabrielle Union | Steve Harvey |
| Trey Songz | Prince | Solange Knowles | Oprah Winfrey |
| Ahmir Khalib Thompson | Rev. Al Sharpton | Viola Davis | Eva Pigford |
| Rihanna | Jill Scott | Kendrick Lamar | Brandy |

*NOTE—Include someone with braided hair

Prior to the start of the session, display the numbered pictures on a wall, table or the floor.

1. Give each participant the handout, Good and Bad Hair.
2. Read the directions together, and direct participants to set out on their Hair Journey.
3. After viewing and classifying the photos/images, have students return to their seats.
4. Begin a discussion using the following questions:
   - What is your definition of good hair? Who has good hair? How did you come to your conclusion?
   - What is your definition of bad hair? Who has bad hair? How did you come to your conclusion?
   - What type of hair do you have in its natural state? Explain your reasoning.
5. Pass out paper, pens, and markers.
6. Introduce the Hair Story Timeline.

### Leader's Notes—Hair Story Timeline

Each student will create a Hair Story Timeline. The timeline should identify ages and stages and personal feelings about your hair. Review verse 1 of I am Not My Hair as an example. Prior to the session create your own Hair Story Timeline for participants to see and understand the concept. Before students begin work, review verse 1 of the song.

~How to Create a Hair Story Timeline~

- ✓ Take a piece of paper 8.5x11 or 8.5x14.
- ✓ Draw a line down the middle of the paper, either horizontally or vertically.
- ✓ Think about the different hairstyles you've worn over the years.
- ✓ List the styles that correspond with your age.
- ✓ See the following example.

**Hair Story Timeline**

| Birth | Age 5 | Age 8 | Age 13 | Age 16 |
|---|---|---|---|---|
| Born with curly hair | pressed hair wore ribbons/bows | Afro-puffs natural styles | relaxer bob-haircut | sew-in weave down my back |

Use this example to help you create your own hair story timeline. Consider making it personally creative by using colors, illustrations, etc.

7. Share your personal Hair Story Timeline.
8. Give participants time to create.
9. After working, give participants time to share their Hair Story Timeline with a partner.
10. After sharing, ask the following questions:
    - What words would you use to describe your hair story? Why did you choose these words?
    - Has your hair story been a positive one or mostly negative? Explain.
    - Why are discussions about Black hair painful and controversial?
    - How do you feel about your hair right now? Explain.
11. Continue by saying, "India says, I am not my hair, I am not this skin, I am not your expectations." What do you think this means? Why is this phrase significant?
12. To close the session, have students repeat after you, "I am not my hair, I am not this skin, I am a soul that lives within."
13. Extinguish the candle.

## SESSION TWO—A HAIR JOURNEY

### SET-UP

**(You'll need an Afrocentric cloth, large jar candle, candle lighter)**

1. On a table place a piece of Afrocentric cloth and a large jar candle.
2. Begin by saying, "We light this candle and ask God's presence to be with us as we study and take a hair journey that will inform, enlighten and encourage us to love the hair that God has blessed us with. In Jesus name, Amen".
3. Light the candle. continue the session with "ENGAGING."

### ENGAGING

**(You'll need Bibles, pens, pencils, and journals)**

1. Say to participants, "India says, I am not my hair, I am not this skin, I am not your expectations, I am not my hair, I am not this skin, I am a soul that lives within."
2. Follow up by asking, "Have you ever felt that your hair defined who you are, and that you had to live up to people's expectations? Explain.".
3. Ask, "What does it mean that you are a soul that lives within?"
4. Tell participants to open their bibles and turn to 1 Samuel 16:7. Select one participant to read.

[7] But the Lord said to Samuel, "Do not consider his appearance or his height, for I have rejected him. The Lord does not look at the things people look at. People look at the outward appearance, but the Lord looks at the heart."

5. After reading ask the following questions:
   - What message do you take away from this verse?
   - How does this verse connect with India's words, "I am a soul that lives within?"
   - Do you ever have conflicting thoughts about who you are on the inside versus your outward appearance? How do you deal with those thoughts?
6. Tell participants to open their bibles and turn to 1 Peter 3: 3-4. Select one participant to read.

[3] Your beauty should not come from outward adornment, such as elaborate hairstyles and the wearing of gold jewelry or fine clothes. [4] Rather, it should be that of your inner self, the unfading beauty of a gentle and quiet spirit, which is of great worth in God's sight.

7. After reading ask the following questions:
   - What is the passage saying?
   - What would you rather have outward beauty (makeup), elaborate hairstyles, gold jewelry, fine clothes or a beauty that never fades from the inside, the beauty of a gentle and quiet spirit

which is of great worth in God's sight? Why? Which one is valued over the other? What happens when we put too much emphasis on outer beauty and neglect our inner beauty? Is it possible to have both inner and outer beauty? Explain.

- Put 1 Peter 3: 3-4 in conversation with the song "I am Not My Hair." How do the messages complement or contradict each other?
- What personal message do you take away from "I Am Not My Hair and the scripture passages? What difference will this message make in your life? Write your response in your journal.

**EXPLORING**

**(You'll need the DVD *School Daze* by Spike Lee— scene 7—"Straight and Nappy" or the YouTube video, "School daze . good and bad hair" (6:08) or choose from the DVD *Good Hair* by Chris Rock— scenes 2 and 3 (Sit Back and Relax, Burn of the Perm) [11:00-25:00], the Straight & Nappy Handout- p .197, pens, pencils, journals) Choose either the Option 1 from *School Daze* or Option 2 from *Good Hair* to complete the following activities)**

1. Choose from Option 1 or Option 2 below.

**Option 1: School Daze (Good and Bad Hair/Straight & Nappy)**

1. Distribute the Straight & Nappy handout to each participant.
2. Read the directions.
3. Watch the video together.
4. After viewing, have students gather in pairs to complete the handout.
5. Review the handout.
6. Ask the following questions about the video:
    - In the video, how do the wannabes and jigaboos define each other? (Suggested answers—Wannabe=better than me, Jigaboo=trying to find something to do)
    - What does this say about their relationship with each other? (Suggested answers—Jigaboos believes the Wannabes think they are superior, Wannabes believe that the Jigaboos lack purpose or are unproductive.
    - After viewing the video, please describe how hair type is related to skin type?
    - In the video, the following phrase was mentioned, "I Don't Mind Being Black," as it relates to the Jigaboos. In your opinion, does the desire to wear long hair or weave denote the idea of not wanting to be black?
    - How was dance used as a means of expression for each group? How did each group demonstrate pride in their hair type/skin tone?
    - After viewing the video, what are your thoughts about straight and nappy hair?
    - Black people's self-esteem is wrapped up in their hair. Do you agree? Why? Why not?

**Straight and Nappy**

The scene "Straight and Nappy," from the film *School Daze* by Spike Lee was produced in 1988. It was partly based on Spike Lee's experiences as a student at Morehouse College in Atlanta, Georgia. It touches on the issue of good hair and bad hair within the African American community.

Share this with the participants: "Prior to the scene in the beauty salon, the young women who were both light skinned and dark skinned exchanged some words in the hallway. Work with a partner to define the following terms":

- **MISS THING**: (A sarcastic term for conceited, puffed up women who think they are really something when they are not)
- **PICKANINNY**: (An offensive, derogatory term for dark skinned Black children)
- **BARBIE DOLL**: (A light skinned girl who is fake and thinks she is better than everyone)
- **HIGH YELLOW HEIFER**: (A Black person with very light skin thought of as a female cow)
- **TAR BABY**: (An African American who is very dark)
- **WANNABE WHITE** ( A person who tries to act White)
- **JIGABOO**: (A really dark skinned Black person with strong features—big lips, wide nose, nappy hair)

Discuss the following questions with your partner:

- What are your thoughts about these terms? Have you ever been called one of these names? How did you feel? Explain.

**Option 2: Good Hair (2. Sit Back and Relax & 3. Burn of the Perm)**

1. Start this segment by saying, "Comedian Chris Rock created a movie about Black Hair in 2009. His motivation to produce this film stemmed from a question his young daughter asked him, 'Daddy how come I don't have good hair?' He set out on a journey to find out what good hair really is."
2. Show scenes 2 and 3 from Good Hair.
3. Encourage the participants to take notes about what they find to be interesting.
4. After watching, ask the following questions:
   - What did you learn about Black hair and Black hair care?
   - Who is Mr. Dudley? Why is he significant to the hair care industry?
   - Why do men, women and children get perms/relaxers knowing the damage it could cause?
   - When is it too young to get a relaxer?
   - Were you surprised to learn that men get perms/relaxers too? Explain.
   - What do you prefer, permed/relaxed or natural hair? Please share.

- How would you help someone understand the reason why some people get relaxers when there is pain and possible skin and hair damage involved? You are not trying to convince them to get a relaxer, just help them understand some people's reasoning. Act it out with a small group.
- Black people's self-esteem is wrapped up in their hair. Do you agree? Why? Why not?

2. To close the session, gather in a circle and have participants repeat after you. "I am not my hair, I am not this skin, I am not your expectations."
3. Extinguish the candle.

## SESSION THREE—A HAIR JOURNEY

### SET-UP

**(You'll need an Afrocentric cloth, large jar candle, candle lighter)**

1. On a table place a piece of Afrocentric cloth and a large jar candle.
2. Begin by saying, "We light this candle and ask God's presence to be with us as we study and take a hair journey that will inform, enlighten and encourage us to love the hair that God has blessed us with. In Jesus name," Amen".
3. Light the candle. Continue the session with "EMERGING."

### EMERGING

**(You'll need journals, pens, paper, markers, and pencils)**

**Leader's Notes—Paying Homage**

Homage is respect or reverence paid to something. Students are asked to produce a creative work—"Homage to Black Hair." It could be a poem, spoken word piece, portrait, essay, etc. that pays tribute to Black hair or their hair in particular. Reflect on the conversations, lyrics, scripture, Hair Story timeline, and videos for inspiration.

1. Encourage students to take out their journals, paper, pencils, markers.
2. Introduce the "Homage to Black Hair" activity.
3. Allow students to collaborate and begin work. (Most likely they will not complete the assignment. Encourage them to continue to work at home, and bring their finished work to the next session.)

### HONORING

**(You'll need index cards that were used during INVITING, pens, and pencils)**

1. Start by saying, "Good hair is all hair that God has created. All of us have been created in God's image. After creating us, God said, "Now, that's good." Therefore everything about me is good, my hair and all."
2. On the blank side of the index card, have participants write a statement about their hair.
3. Continue by asking, "Has your perception of good and bad hair changed? How? Please share".
4. After sharing, close the session with the following prayer.

God, we thank you for the opportunity to share in this experience and learn about our hair and our beauty. Thank you God for looking at our hearts, not our outward appearance. Help us to realize that you call us to love ourselves, to love you and our neighbors. Thank you God, that I am not my hair. In Jesus Name, Amen.

# "A Hair Journey" Handouts

**~good hair—bad hair~**

Take a journey through the valley of "complicated, complex, and questionable hair." Take a good look at the hairstyles you see. Would you describe them as good, bad or something else? Number your paper according to the number of pictures there are. Classify each hairstyle as either good hair or bad hair. Write your responses on your paper. When you are finished, return to your seat. Make sure that you are able to elaborate on your choices.

## STRAIGHT AND NAPPY

The scene "Straight and Nappy," from the film *School Daze* by Spike Lee was produced in 1988. It was partly based on Spike Lee's experiences as a student at Morehouse College in Atlanta, Georgia. It touches on the issue of good hair and bad hair within the African American community.

Prior to the scene in the beauty salon, the young women who were both light skinned and dark skinned exchanged some words in the hallway. Work with a partner to define the following terms used in the movie clip.

- MISS THING:
- PICKANINNY:
- BARBIE DOLL:
- HIGH YELLOW HEIFER:
- TAR BABY:
- JIGABOO:

Discuss the following questions with your partner:

- What are your thoughts about these terms?
- Have you ever been called one of these names?
- How did you feel? Explain.

# Bibliography


Armstong, T. *Multiple Intelligences in the Classroom*. Alexandria: Association of Curriculum and Supervision Development, 1994.

Arthur, Kay, David Arthur and Pete DeLacy. *The New How to Study Your Bible: Discover the Life Changing Approach to God's Word*. Eugene: Harvest House, 2010.

Baker Dori, *Girlfriend Theology: God-Talk with Young Women*. Cleveland: The Pilgrim Press, 2005.

Baker, Soren. *The History of Rap and Hip-Hop*. New York: Lucent, 2006.

Bass, Dorothy and Don Richter. *Way to Live: Leader's Guide—Ideas for Growing in Christian Practices With Teens*. Nashville: Upper Room, 2002.

Blanks, Andy. *The 7 Best Practices for Teaching Teenagers the Bible*. United States: Youth Ministry 360, 2012.

Breitman, George editor. *Malcolm X Speaks*. New York: Grove Press, 1966.

Brown, Teresa L. Fry. *God Don't Like Ugly: African American Women Handing on Spiritual Values*. Nashville: Abingdon Press, 2000.

Bryant, Thema Simone. *The Birthing of a Lioness: A Collection of Poems and Prophecies*. Washington, D.C.: Akosua Visions, 1997.

Butler Jr., Lee H. *Liberating Our Dignity, Saving Our Souls*. St. Louis: Chalice Press, 2006.

Calhoun, Adele. *Spiritual Disciplines Handbook: Practices That Transform Us*. Downer's Gove: Intervarsity, 2005.

Cannon, Katie. *Translating Womanism into Pedagogical Praxis*. Charlotte: University of North Carolina, 1997.

Chuck D. *Fight the Power: Rap, Race and Reality*. New York: Dell Publishing, 1997.

Dockery, Karen. *The Youth Worker's Guide to Creative Bible Study—Revised and Expanded*. Nashville: Broadman and Hollman Publishers, 1999.

Dyson, Michael Eric. "The Culture of Hip-Hop" in *The Michael Eric Dyson Reader*. New York: Basic Civitas, 2004.

Fleming, Robert. *Wisdom of the Elders*. New York: Ballantine Books, 1996.

Floyd Jr., Samuel A. *The Power of Black Music: Interpreting Its History From Africa to the United States*. New York: Oxford University Press, 1995.

Foster, Richard. *Celebration of Discipline*. San Francisco: Harper Collins, 1998.

Gardner, Howard. *Multiple Intelligences: Theory and Practice*. New York: Basic Books, 1993.

Gill, Megan Murphy. "Selfie-Esteem." in *US Catholic*, September 2014.

Hollies, Linda. *Mother Goose Meets a Woman Called Wisdom. A Short Discourse in the Art of Self Determination*. Cleveland: United Church Press, 2000.

hooks, bell. *Killing Rage: Ending Racism*. New York: Henry Holt, 1995.

hooks, bell. *Teaching to Transgress: Education as the Practice of Freedom*. New York: Vintage, 1994.

Howard, Marion, Marie Mitchell and Sharon Nieb. Media Madness: An Educational Series for Parents. Atlanta: Emory University, 2008.Atlanta: Emory University, 2008.

Karenga, Maulana. *Kwanzaa: A Celebration of Family, Community and Culture*. Los Angeles: University of Sankore Press, 1998.

Lambert, Dan. *Teaching that Makes a Difference: How to Teach for Holistic Impact*. Grand Rapids: Zondervan, 2004.

LeFever, Marlene. *Leaning Styles: Reaching Everyone God Gave You to Teach*. Colorado Springs: Nex/Gen/Cook Communications Ministries, 2004.

Lucado, Max and Randy Freeze. *The Story: The Bible as One Continuing Story of God and His People*. Grand Rapids: Zondervan, 2011.

Mears, Henrietta C. *What the Bible is All About*. Ventura: Regal Books, 1997.

Nasir, Na'llah, Suad. *Racialized Identities: Race & African American Achievement Among African American Youth*. Stanford: Stanford University Press, 2012.

Niebuhr, H. Richard. *Christ and Culture—Fiftieth Anniversary Expanded Edition*. New York: Harper Collins, 2001.

Outcalt. Todd. *Show Me the Way: 50 Bible Study Ideas for Youth*. (Nashville: Abingdon Press, 2000.

Parker, Evelyn L. *Trouble Don't Last Always: Emancipatory Hope among African American Adolescents*. Cleveland: The Pilgrim Press, 2003.

Pinn, Anthony. *Why Lord? Suffering and Evil in Black Theology,* New York: Continuum, 1999.

Porter, Michael. *Rap and the Eroticizing of Black Youth*. Chicago: African American Images, 2006.

Price, Emmett G. Executive Editor. *Encyclopedia of African American Music—Volume 3: P-Z*. Santa Barbara: Greenwood, 2011.

Riley, Dorothy Winbush. *The Complete Kwanzaa: Celebrating Our Cultural Harvest*. New York: Harper Collins, 1995.

Saliers, Don and Emily. *A Song to Sing: A Life to Live*. San Francisco: Jossey Bass, 2005.

Shockley, Grant. "Christian Education and the Black Church: A Contextual Approach" in *Journal of Interdenominational Theological Center*, Spring 1975.

Shockley Grant. "Christian Education and the Black Religious Experience," in *Ethnicity in the Education of the Church,* edited by Charles Foster. Nashville: Scarritt, 1987.

Smith, Yolanda. *Reclaiming the Spirituals: New Possibilities for African American Christian Education*. Cleveland: The Pilgrim Press, 2004.

West, Cornel. *Brother West: Living and Loving Out Loud*. New York City: Hay House Inc., 2009.

Westing, Harold and Penny Thome. *Building Biblical Values: Innovative Learning Exercises for All Ages*. Grand Rapids: Kregel, 1996.

Wimberly, Anne E. Streaty and Evelyn L. Parker. *In Search of Wisdom: Faith Formation in the Black Church*. Nashville: Abingdon Press, 2002.

Wimberly, Anne E. Streaty. *Keep It Real: Working with Today's Black Youth*. Nashville: Abingdon Press, 2005.

Wimberly, Anne E. Streaty and Evelyn L. Parker. *Nurturing Faith and Hope: Black Worship as a Model For Christian Education*. Cleveland: The Pilgrim Press, 2004.

Wimberly, Anne E. Streaty. *Soul Stories: African American Christian Education—Revised Edition*. Nashville: Abingdon Press, 2005.

Zacharias, Ravi. "An Ancient Message, Through Modern Means, to a Postmodern Mind," in *Truth Telling*. Grand Rapids: Zondervan, 2000.

# Endnotes

**Introduction**

1 Throughout the book, the terms African American and Black will be used interchangeably.

2 James 1:2-8, New Living Translation.

3 Quote Investigator: Exploring the Origins of Quotations. http://www.quoteinvestigator.com. Accessed January 22, 2016.

4 Ravi Zacharias, "An Ancient Message, Through Modern Means, to a Postmodern Mind," in Telling the Truth, ed. D.A. Carson (Grand Rapids: Zondervan, 2000), p.26

5 Mark 10:13-16. The Message.

**Chapter One**

6 Steven Covey. Brainy Quote.com, Xplore Inc, 2015. http://brainyquote.com/quotes/quotes/stevencov636532.html, accessed November 5, 2015.

7 http://lifelock.com.

8 Genesis 1:27. *The VOICE Reader's Bible* (Nashville: Thomas Nelson Publishers, 2012), 2.

9 Megan Murphy Gill. "Selfie Esteem." US Catholic, September 2014, 18.

10 Cornel West. *Brother West: Living and Loving Out Loud.* (New York City: Hay House Inc, 2009), 148.

11 Reference to Ephesians 2: 8-10. I use this description to identify young Black Christians called by God to walk in their purpose.

12 Michael Porter, *Rap and the Eroticizing of Black Youth.* (Chicago: African American Images), vi.

13 Anthony B. Pinn, *Why Lord? Suffering and Evil in Black Theology* (New York: Continuum, 1999), 125.

14 Soren Baker. *The History of Rap and Hip-Hop* (New York: Lucent, 2006), 28.

15 Michael Eric Dyson. *"The Culture of Hip-Hop" in The Michael Eric Dyson Reader (*New York: Basic Civitas, 2004), 402.

16 Chuck D. *Fight the Power: Rap, Race and Reality* (New York: Dell Publishing, 1997), 256.

17 Lee H. Butler, Jr., *Liberating our Dignity, Saving our Souls* (St. Louis: Chalice Press, 2006), 14

18 Lee H. Butler, Jr., *Liberating our Dignity, Saving our Souls* (St. Louis: Chalice Press, 2006), 11.

19 bell hooks, *Killing Rage: Ending Racism* (New York: Henry Holt, 1995), 114.

20 Dictionary.reference.com. http:://www.dictionary.com "stereotype" Accessed November 21, 2015.

21 Na'Ilah Suad Nasir. *Racialized Identities: Race and African American Achievement Among African American Youth* (Stanford: Stanford University Press, 2012), 62.

22 Malachi 3:6. The Holy Bible-Today's New International Version (Grand Rapids: Zondervan, 2005)

23 Psalm 139: 1, 7, 13-14, 16. New International Version.

24 1 Peter 5:8 The Holy Bible. Today's New International Version (Grand Rapids: Zondervan, 2005)

**Chapter Two**

25 Marcus Garvey. BrainyQuote.com, Xplore Inc, 2015. http://www.brainyquote.com/quotes/quotes/m/garv.365148.html, accessed Oct 22, 2015

26 E.J. Bassette, *"Part 3 of 5—Interview with author, Donna Bassette on "In the Kitchen"—Dawson Twins By Way of Egypt—Tales of the Ancestors Voices by Donna Bassette,* YouTube Video. http//www.youtube.com/watch?v=vauDwqNik2m. Accessed October 23, 2015.

27 Michael J. Feeney. "Harlem and Malcolm X's daughter slam Nicki Minaj for online artwork , that they call 'disrespectful'. NY Daily News. Accessed October 23,, 2015.http://www.nydailynews.com/new-york/uptown/local-harlem-leaders-fed-minaj-article/.

28 Biography.com Editors, "Emmet Till Biography. " *Biography.com*. Accessed October 23, 2015. http://www.biography.com/people/emmett-till-507515.

29 R.J. Cubarrubia, "Little Wayne Apologizes for Inappropriate Emmett Till Lyric." *Rollingstone.com*. Accessed October 23, 2015. http://www.rollingstone.com/music/news/lil-wayne-apologizes-for-inappropriate-emmett-till-lyric-20130501#1xzz3pK2tLbF3.

30 "Harriet Tubman Sex Tape: Russell Simmons issues Apology for Controversial Parody." *Huffingtonpost.com*. Accessed, October 23, 2015. http://www.huffingtonpost.com/2013/8/15/harriet-tubman-sex-tape-russell-simmons-issues-apology/

31 Dion Rabouin. Black History Has Been an Epic Failure—the Blog. Huff Post Black Voices. http://www.huffingtonpost.com/dion-babouin/black-history-month_b_2581805.htm Accessed February 2, 2016.

32 http://www.berea.edu/cgwc/the-power-of-sankofa.

33 Sherry Estrada. "McGraw-Hill CEO Apologizes for Textbook 'Mistake' on Slavery." *Diversityinc.com*. Accessed on October 22, 2015. http://www.diversityinc.com/news/mcgraw-hill-ceo-apologizes-for-textbook-mistake-on-slavery.

34 "Africans in America—The Growth of Slavery in North America." *PBS.org*. Accessed October 24, 2015. http://pbs.org/wgbh/aia/part1/narr5.html.

## Chapter Three

35 Susan L. Taylor. Ibtimes.com. "Black History Month 2014: 30, Inspirational Quotes from Black American Leaders," accessed December 21, 2015.

36 Names of students have been changed to protect identity.

37 Dorothy Winbush Riley. *The Complete Kwanzaa: Celebrating Our Cultural Harvest*. (New York: Harper Collins, 1995), 3.

38 Marion Howard, Marie Mitchell, Sharon Nieb. *Media Madness: An Educational Series for Parents*. (Atlanta: Emory University, 2008), 74.

39 Beth Chee. "Today's Teens: More Materialistic, Less Willing to Work" http://www.newscenter.sdsu.edu. Accessed December 21, 2015.

40 Beth Chee. "Today's Teens: More Materialistic, Less Willing to Work" http://www.newscenter.sdsu.edu. Accessed December 21, 2015.

41 Maulana Karenga. *Kwanzaa: A Celebration of Family, Community and Culture*. (Los Angeles: University of Sankore Press, 1998), 34.

42 Maulana Karenga. *Kwanzaa: A Celebration of Family, Community and Culture*. (Los Angeles: University of Sankore Press, 1998).

43 Dorothy Winbush Riley. "Row Together: Proverbs for Umoja," *The Complete Kwanzaa: Celebrating Our Cultural Harvest*. (New York: Harper Collins, 1995), 65-66.

44 Maulana Karenga. *Kwanzaa: A Celebration of Family, Community and Culture*. (Los Angeles: University of Sankore Press, 1998), 34.

45 Maulana Karenga. *Kwanzaa: A Celebration of Family, Community and Culture*. (Los Angeles: University of Sankore Press, 1998), 50.

46 Maulana Karenga. *Kwanzaa: A Celebration of Family, Community and Culture*. (Los Angeles: University of Sankore Press, 1998).

47 Dorothy Winbush Riley. *The Complete Kwanzaa: Celebrating Our Cultural Harvest*. (New York: Harper Collins, 1995), 71.

48 Maulana Karenga. *Kwanzaa: A Celebration of Family, Community and Culture*. (Los Angeles: University of Sankore Press, 1998) 34.

49 Maulana Karenga. *Kwanzaa: A Celebration of Family, Community and Culture*. (Los Angeles: University of Sankore Press, 1998), 53.

50 Dorothy Winbush Riley. *The Complete Kwanzaa: Celebrating Our Cultural Harvest*. (New York: Harper Collins, 1995), 118.

51 Maulana Karenga. *Kwanzaa: A Celebration of Family, Community and Culture*. (Los Angeles: University of Sankore Press, 1998), 34.

52 Dorothy Winbush Riley. *The Complete Kwanzaa: Celebrating Our Cultural Harvest*. (New York: Harper Collins, 1995), 172.

53 Maulana Karenga. *Kwanzaa: A Celebration of Family, Community and Culture*. (Los Angeles: University of Sankore Press, 1998), 59.

54 Maulana Karenga. *Kwanzaa: A Celebration of Family, Community and Culture*. (Los Angeles: University of Sankore Press, 1998),34.

55 Maulana Karenga. *Kwanzaa: A Celebration of Family, Community and Culture*. (Los Angeles: University of Sankore Press, 1998).

56 Dorothy Winbush Riley. *The Complete Kwanzaa: Celebrating Our Cultural Harvest*. (New York: Harper Collins, 1995), 263.

57 Dorothy Winbush Riley. *The Complete Kwanzaa: Celebrating Our Cultural Harvest*. (New York: Harper Collins, 1995), 281.

58 Mary McLeod Bethune. "Last Will and Testament." http://www.cookman.edu. Accessed December 29, 2015.

**Chapter Four**

59 Afrika Bambaataa & Soulsonic Force, "Planet Rock" Digital Music (Essential Media Group), 2012.

60 Samuel A. Floyd, Jr. *The Power of Black Music: Interpreting Its History from Africa to the United States*. (New York: Oxford University Press, 1995), 14.

61 Emmett G. Price, Executive Editor. *Encyclopedia of African American Music—Volume 3: P-Z* (Santa Barbara: Greenwood, 2011). For a comprehensive exploration of African American music including information on genres, styles, individuals, groups, collectives and historical topics please see *Encyclopedia of African American Music—volumes 1, 2, 3 edited by Emmett G. Price*.

62 Don & Emily Saliers, *A Song to Sing, A Life to Live* (San Francisco: Jossey Bass, 2005), 73.

63 Don & Emily Saliers, *A Song to Sing, A Life to Live* (San Francisco: Jossey Bass, 2005), 1.

64 Don & Emily Saliers, *A Song to Sing, A Life to Live* (San Francisco: Jossey Bass, 2005), 73.

65 India.Arie. "I Am Not My Hair," Digital Music (Universal), 2005.

66 The Game. "Don't Shoot," Digital Music (Mike Brown), 2014.

67 Faith Evans. "Lovin' Me," Digital Music (eOne Music) 2012.

68 Samuel A. Floyd, Jr. *The Power of Black Music: Interpreting Its History from Africa to the United States*. (New York: Oxford University Press, 1995), 136.

**Chapter Five**

69 Psalm 119:9 Holy Bible Large Print Slimline Edition—New Living Translation (Carol Stream: Tyndale House Publishers, 2012).

70 Will L. Thompson. "Jesus is all the World to Me (Copyright Public Domain) 1904.

71 The Apostle's Creed (Copyright Public Domain).

72 Henrietta C. Mears. *What the Bible is All About* (Ventura: Regal Books. 1997), 9.

73 Max Lucado and Randy Freeze. *The Story: The Bible as One Continuing Story of God and His People* (Grand Rapids: Zondervan, 2011), vii.

74 Jack Wellman. "5 Tips for Picking the Best Bible Translation." http.www.whatchristianswant-toknow.com" Accessed November 29, 2015.

75 Jack Wellman. "5 Tips for Picking the Best Bible Translation." http.www.whatchristianswant-toknow.com" Accessed November 29, 2015.

76 Andy Blanks. *The 7 Best Practices for Teaching Teenagers the Bible* (United States: Youth Ministry 360, 2012), 55.

77 Andy Blanks. *The 7 Best Practices for Teaching Teenagers the Bible* (United States: Youth Ministry 360, 2012), 56.

78 Andy Blanks. *The 7 Best Practices for Teaching Teenagers the Bible* (United States: Youth Ministry 360, 2012), 56.

79 Andy Blanks. *The 7 Best Practices for Teaching Teenagers the Bible* (United States: Youth Ministry 360, 2012), 56.

80 Andy Blanks. *The 7 Best Practices for Teaching Teenagers the Bible* (United States: Youth Ministry 360, 2012), 58.

81 Kay Arthur, David Arthur, Pete DeLacy. *The New How to Study Your Bible: Discover the Life Changing Approach to God's Word,* (Eugene: Harvest House Publishers, 2010), 8.

82 Kay Arthur, David Arthur, Pete DeLacy. *The New How to Study Your Bible: Discover the Life Changing Approach to God's Word,* (Eugene: Harvest House Publishers, 2010), 10.

83 Kay Arthur, David Arthur, Pete DeLacy. *The New How to Study Your Bible: Discover the Life Changing Approach to God's Word,* (Eugene: Harvest House Publishers, 2010), 11.

84 Kay Arthur, David Arthur, Pete DeLacy. *The New How to Study Your Bible: Discover the Life Changing Approach to God's Word,* (Eugene: Harvest House Publishers, 2010), 12.

85 Kay Arthur, David Arthur, Pete DeLacy. *The New How to Study Your Bible: Discover the Life Changing Approach to God's Word,* (Eugene: Harvest House Publishers, 2010), 12.

86 Resources about the Inductive Bible Study Method can be found at (http://www.intothyword.org).

87 Consider using *Bible Passage as Script, Mystery Question and Read with Tools* from Karen Dockery. *The Youth Worker's Guide to Creative Bible Study—Revised and Expanded* (Nashville: Broadman and Hollman Publishers, 1999).

88 Karen Dockery. *The Youth Worker's Guide to Creative Bible Study—Revised and Expanded* (Nashville: Broadman and Hollman Publishers, 1999), 35.

89 Karen Dockery. *The Youth Worker's Guide to Creative Bible Study—Revised and Expanded* (Nashville: Broadman and Hollman Publishers, 1999), 36-37.

90 Karen Dockery. *The Youth Worker's Guide to Creative Bible Study—Revised and Expanded* (Nashville: Broadman and Hollman Publishers, 1999), 36-37.

91 Todd Outcalt. *Show Me the Way: 50 Bible Study Ideas for Youth* (Nashville: Abingdon Press, 2000), 18.

92 Todd Outcalt. *Show Me the Way: 50 Bible Study Ideas for Youth* (Nashville: Abingdon Press, 2000), 32.

93 Todd Outcalt. *Show Me the Way: 50 Bible Study Ideas for Youth* (Nashville: Abingdon Press, 2000), 22.

**Chapter Six**

94 Spoken by Black Nationalist Leader Malcolm X from a 1964 speech. George Breitman, ed. *Malcolm X Speaks* (New York: Grove Press, 1966), 136.

95 Robert Fleming. *Wisdom of the Elders.* (New York: Ballantine Books, 1996), xv-xvi.

96 Ecclesiastes 1:9.

97 Introduction to Ecclesiastes, *The New Interpreters Study Bible—New Revised Standard Version with the Apocrypha* (Nashville: Abingdon Press, 2003), 929

98 Spotlight on Ecclesiastes. *NIV Essentials Study Bible* (Grand Rapids: Zondervan, 2013), 793.

99 Linda H. Hollies. *Mother Goose Meets A Woman Called Wisdom: A Short Discourse in the Art of Self-Determination* (Cleveland: United Church Press, 2000), 2.

100 Proverbs 8: 22-23 (New Revised Standard Version).

101 Conversation with Dr. Anne Streaty Wimberly, focusing on the question "What is wisdom?" June 11, 2007. This in person conversation was held at the Simpsonwood Conference Center in Norcross, Georgian at the 2007 Hope Builders Residential Program. This perspective on wisdom also appears in the Introduction of Anne E. Streaty Wimberly and Evelyn L. Parker, eds. *In Search of Wisdom: Faith Formation in the Black Church* (Nashville: Abingdon, 2002), 11-21.

102 Wimberly and Evelyn L. Parker, eds. *In Search of Wisdom: Faith Formation in the Black Church* (Nashville: Abingdon, 2002), 12-13.

103 Thema Simone Bryant. *The Birthing of a Lioness: A Collection of Poems and Prophecies* (Washington DC: Akosua Visions, 1997), 97-98.

104 Proverbs 22:6 (New Living Translation)

105 bell hooks. *Teaching to Transgress: Education as the Practice of Freedom* (New York: Vintage, 1994), 13.

106 Wimberly and Parker, 12-13.

107 Grant Shockley, "Christian Education and the Black Church: A Contextual Approach," *Journal of the Interdenominational Theological Center* (Spring 1975): 75-88.

108 Grant Shockley, "Christian Education and the Black Religious Experience," Charles Foster, ed. *Ethnicity in the Education of the Church* (Nashville: Scarritt, 1987), 41.

109 Grant Shockley, "Christian Education and the Black Religious Experience," Charles Foster, ed. *Ethnicity in the Education of the Church* (Nashville: Scarritt, 1987), 41.

110 Grant Shockley, "Christian Education and the Black Religious Experience," Charles Foster, ed. *Ethnicity in the Education of the Church* (Nashville: Scarritt, 1987), 41.

111 Grant Shockley, "Christian Education and the Black Religious Experience," Charles Foster, ed. *Ethnicity in the Education of the Church* (Nashville: Scarritt, 1987), 41.

112 Grant Shockley, "Christian Education and the Black Religious Experience," Charles Foster, ed. *Ethnicity in the Education of the Church* (Nashville: Scarritt, 1987), 41.

113 Yolanda Smith. *Reclaiming the Spirituals: New Possibilities for African American Christian Education,* (Cleveland: Pilgrim, 2004), viii.

114 Yolanda Smith. "Forming Wisdom through Cultural Rootedness," Anne E. Streaty Wimberly and Evelyn L. Parker, *In Search of Wisdom: Faith Formation in the Black Church* (Nashville: Abingdon Press, 2002), 51.

115 Yolanda Smith. *Reclaiming the Spirituals: New Possibilities for African American Christian Education,* (Cleveland: Pilgrim, 2004), 17-20.

116 Anne Streaty Wimberly. *Soul Stories: African American Christian Education—Revised Edition* (Nashville: Abingdon Press, 2005),

**Chapter Seven**

117 Anne Streaty Wimberly. *Soul Stories: African American Christian Education—Revised Edition* (Nashville: Abingdon Press, 2005),xi

118 Anne Streaty Wimberly. *Soul Stories: African American Christian Education—Revised Edition* (Nashville: Abingdon Press, 2005), 26-34.

119 Lora Ellen McKinney. *Christian Education in the African American Church: A Guide for Teaching Truth* (Valley Forge: Judson Press, 2003), 3.

120 Anne Wimberly. *Nurturing Faith and Hope: Black Worship as a Model for Christian Education* (Cleveland: Pilgrim Press, 2004), 6.

121 Anne Wimberly. *Nurturing Faith and Hope: Black Worship as a Model for Christian Education* (Cleveland: Pilgrim Press, 2004), 7-11.

122 Matthew 7: 12 (New Living Translation).

123 2 Corinthians 5: 17 (New Living Translation).

124 Harold J. Westing and Penny Thome. *Building Biblical Values: Innovative Learning Exercises for All Ages* (Grand Rapids: Kregel, 1996), 8.

125 Harold J. Westing and Penny Thome. *Building Biblical Values: Innovative Learning Exercises for All Ages* (Grand Rapids: Kregel, 1996), 15-20.

126 Yolanda Y. Smith & Mary Elizabeth Mullino Moore, "Olivia Pearl Stokes: A Living Testimony of Faith," Barbara Anne Keely, ed. *Faith of Our Foremothers: Women Changing Religious Education* (Louisville: John Knox, 1997), 106.

127 Yolanda Y. Smith & Mary Elizabeth Mullino Moore, "Olivia Pearl Stokes: A Living Testimony of Faith," Barbara Anne Keely, ed. *Faith of Our Foremothers: Women Changing Religious Education* (Louisville: John Knox, 1997), 106.

**Chapter Eight**

128 Craig Dykstra, "Practicing Our Faith," *The Valparaiso Project on the Education and Formation of People,* 2006-2011, June 23, 2015, http:www.practicingourfaith.org.

129 Dorothy Bass and Don Richter, *Way to Live: Leader's Guide—Ideas for Growing in Christian Practices with Teens* (Nashville: Upper Room, 2002), 10-11.

130 Richard J. Foster, *Celebration of Discipline* (San Francisco: Harper Collins, 1998), 63-64.

131 Adele Ahlberg Calhoun, *Spiritual Disciplines Handbook: Practices that Transform Us* (Downers Grove: Intervarsity, 2005), 165.

132 Dorothy Bass and Don Richter, *Way to Live: Leader's Guide—Ideas for Growing in Christian Practices with Teens* (Nashville: Upper Room, 2002), 13-14.

133 Dorothy Bass and Don Richter, *Way to Live: Leader's Guide—Ideas for Growing in Christian Practices with Teens* (Nashville: Upper Room, 2002),.

134 Wimberly, *Soul Stories,* xi.

135 Adele Ahlberg Calhoun, *Spiritual Disciplines Handbook: Practices that Transform Us* (Downers Grove: Intervarsity, 2005), 203.

136 Luke 11:1 (New International Version).

137 Anne E. Streaty Wimberly, *Nurturing Faith and Hope: Black Worship as a Model for Christian Education.* (Cleveland: The Pilgrim Press, 2004), 156.

138 Richard J. Foster, *Celebration of Discipline* (San Francisco: Harper Collins, 1998), 158.

139 Anne E. Streaty Wimberly, *Nurturing Faith and Hope: Black Worship as a Model for Christian Education.* (Cleveland: The Pilgrim Press, 2004), xi.

140 Adele Ahlberg Calhoun, *Spiritual Disciplines Handbook: Practices that Transform Us* (Downers Grove: Intervarsity, 2005), 143.

141 Matt. 20:25-28 (New International Version).

142 James 2:1-26 (New International Version).

143 Yolanda Smith, *Reclaiming The Spirituals: New Possibilities for African American Christian Education* (Cleveland: The Pilgrim Press, 2004), 46.

144 Yolanda Smith, *Reclaiming The Spirituals: New Possibilities for African American Christian Education* (Cleveland: The Pilgrim Press, 2004), 46.

145 Yolanda Smith, *Reclaiming The Spirituals: New Possibilities for African American Christian Education* (Cleveland: The Pilgrim Press, 2004), 46.

146 Evelyn L. Parker, *Trouble Don't Last Always: Emancipatory Hope Among African American Adolescents,* (Cleveland: The Pilgrim Press, 2003), 153.

147 Evelyn L. Parker, *Trouble Don't Last Always: Emancipatory Hope Among African American Adolescents,* (Cleveland: The Pilgrim Press, 2003), 153.

148 Richelle B. White, *Daughters of Imani: Christian Rites of Passage for African American Young Women—Planning Guide,* (Nashville: Abingdon Press, 2005), 21.

149 Anne E. Streaty Wimberly and Maisha Handy, "Conversations on Word and Deed: Forming Wisdom through Female Mentoring", Anne Streaty Wimberly and Evelyn L. Parker, eds. *In Search of Wisdom: Faith Formation in the Black Church* (Nashville: Abingdon, 2002), 109.

150 Anne E. Streaty Wimberly and Maisha Handy, "Conversations on Word and Deed: Forming Wisdom through Female Mentoring", Anne Streaty Wimberly and Evelyn L. Parker, eds. *In Search of Wisdom: Faith Formation in the Black Church* (Nashville: Abingdon, 2002), 109.

151 Wimberly, *Keep It Real: Working with Today's Black Youth* (Nashville: Abingdon Press, 2005), xviii.

**Chapter Nine**

152 Oprah Winfrey, "Thinkexist.com: Oprah Winfrey Quotes" June 16, 2015, http:thinkexist.com

153 Katie Cannon. *Translating Womanism into Pedagogical Praxis.* (Charlotte: University of North Carolina, 1997), 11.

154 Marlene LeFever. *Learning Styles: Reaching Everyone God Gave You to Teach.* (Colorado Springs: NexGen/Cook Communications Ministries, 2004), 40-75.

155 Howard Gardner, *Multiple Intelligences: Theory and Practice.* (New York: Basic Books, 1993), 8-10.

156 T. Armstrong. *Multiple Intelligences in the Classroom* (Alexandria: Association of Curriculum and Supervision Development, 1994)

157 Dan Lambert. *Teaching That Makes a Difference: How to Teach for Holistic Impact* (Grand Rapids: Zondervan, 2004), 141.

158 Dan Lambert. *Teaching That Makes a Difference: How to Teach for Holistic Impact* (Grand Rapids: Zondervan, 2004), 141.

159 Dan Lambert. *Teaching That Makes a Difference: How to Teach for Holistic Impact* (Grand Rapids: Zondervan, 2004), 142-143

160 Dan Lambert. *Teaching That Makes a Difference: How to Teach for Holistic Impact* (Grand Rapids: Zondervan, 2004), 143.

161 Dan Lambert. *Teaching That Makes a Difference: How to Teach for Holistic Impact* (Grand Rapids: Zondervan, 2004), 143.

162 Dan Lambert. *Teaching That Makes a Difference: How to Teach for Holistic Impact* (Grand Rapids: Zondervan, 2004), 144.

163 Dan Lambert. *Teaching That Makes a Difference: How to Teach for Holistic Impact* (Grand Rapids: Zondervan, 2004), 144.

164 Dan Lambert. *Teaching That Makes a Difference: How to Teach for Holistic Impact* (Grand Rapids: Zondervan, 2004), 145.

165 Dan Lambert. *Teaching That Makes a Difference: How to Teach for Holistic Impact* (Grand Rapids: Zondervan, 2004), 145.

166 Dan Lambert. *Teaching That Makes a Difference: How to Teach for Holistic Impact* (Grand Rapids: Zondervan, 2004), 146.

167 Dan Lambert. *Teaching That Makes a Difference: How to Teach for Holistic Impact* (Grand Rapids: Zondervan, 2004), 146.

168 Katie Cannon. *Translating Womanism into Pedagogical Praxis* (Charlotte: University of North Carolina, 1997), 11.

169 Anne Streaty Wimberly. *Nurturing Faith and Hope: Black Worship as a Model for Christian Education*. (Cleveland: The Pilgrim Press, 2004), 146.

170 Dan Lambert. *Teaching that Makes a Difference*. (Grand Rapids: Zondervan, 2004), 142.

171 Ibid., 143.

172 bell hooks. *Teaching to Transgress: Education as the Practice of Freedom* (New York: Vintage Books, 1994), 21.

173 Anthony Pinn. *Why Lord? Suffering and Evil in Black Theology*. New York: Continuum, 2006.

174 Dori Baker. *Girlfriend Theology: God-Talk with Young Women*. (Cleveland: The Pilgrim Press, 2005), 188.

175 Dan Lambert. *Teaching That Makes a Difference: How to Teach for Holistic Impact* (Grand Rapids: Zondervan, 2004), 143.

176 Dan Lambert. *Teaching That Makes a Difference: How to Teach for Holistic Impact* (Grand Rapids: Zondervan, 2004), 143.

**Chapter Ten**

177 https://allthingslearning.wordpress.com/tag/lesson-planning/

**Conclusion**

178 Don Moen, "When It's All Been Said and Done," Digital Music (Integrity Media), 2004.

179 H. Richard Niebuhr. *Christ and Culture—Fiftieth Anniversary Expanded Edition*, (New York: Harper Collins, 2001), 190).

180 H. Richard Niebuhr. *Christ and Culture—Fiftieth Anniversary Expanded Edition*, (New York: Harper Collins, 2001), 190-195).

181 Anthony Brown. "WORTH." Digital Music (B00X572U9G, 2015).

182 Yolanda Adams. "What About the Children." Digital Music (B001386EGC, 1995)

**Appendix A**

183 Smart Goals Guide. wwwsmart-goals-guide.com/smart-goal.html. Accessed April 1, 2016.

184 Smart Goals Guide. wwwsmart-goals-guide.com/smart-goal.html. Accessed April 1, 2016.

**Appendix D**

185 Profiles in Courage and Selma to Montgomery—Three Marches material adapted from biographical information found on History.com. History.com staff. "Selma to Montgomery March" History.com. Accessed October 18, 2015. http://www.history.com/topics/black-history/selma-montgomery-march.

CPSIA information can be obtained
at www.ICGtesting.com
Printed in the USA
FFOW05n0748220716